"After utilizing toolkits from The Art of Service, I was able to identify threats within my organization to which I was completely unaware. Using my team's knowledge as a competitive advantage, we now have superior systems that save time and energy."

"As a new Chief Technology Officer, I was feeling unprepared and inadequate to be successful in my role. I ordered an IT toolkit Sunday night and was prepared Monday morning to shed light on areas of improvement within my organization. I no longer felt overwhelmed and intimidated, I was excited to share what I had learned."

"I used the questionnaires to interview members of my team. I never knew how many insights we could produce collectively with our internal knowledge."

"I usually work until at least 8pm on weeknights. The Art of Service questionnaire saved me so much time and worry that Thursday night I attended my son's soccer game without sacrificing my professional obligations."

"After purchasing The Art of Service toolkit, I was able to identify areas where my company was not in compliance that could have put my job at risk. I looked like a hero when I proactively educated my team on the risks and presented a solid solution."

"I spent months shopping for an external consultant before realizing that The Art of Service would allow my team to consult themselves! Not only did we save time not catching a consultant up to speed, we were able to keep our company information and industry secrets confidential."

"Everyday there are new regulations and processes in my industry. The Art of Service toolkit has kept me ahead by using AI technology to constantly update the toolkits and address emerging needs."

"I customized The Art of Service toolkit to focus specifically on the concerns of my role and industry. I didn't have to waste time with a generic self-help book that wasn't tailored to my exact situation."

"Many of our competitors have asked us about our secret sauce. When I tell them it's the knowledge we have in-house, they never believe me. Little do they know The Art of Service toolkits are working behind the scenes."

"One of my friends hired a consultant who used the knowledge gained working with his company to advise their competitor. Talk about a competitive disadvantage! The Art of Service allowed us to keep our knowledge from walking out the door along with a huge portion of our budget in consulting fees."

"Honestly, I didn't know what I didn't know. Before purchasing The Art of Service, I didn't realize how many areas of my business needed to be refreshed and improved. I am so relieved The Art of Service was there to highlight our blind spots."

"Before The Art of Service, I waited eagerly for consulting company reports to come out each month. These reports kept us up to speed but provided little value because they put our competitors on the same playing field. With The Art of Service, we have uncovered unique insights to drive our business forward."

"Instead of investing extensive resources into an external consultant, we can spend more of our budget towards pursuing our company goals and objectives...while also spending a little more on corporate holiday parties."

"The risk of our competitors getting ahead has been mitigated because The Art of Service has provided us with a 360-degree view of threats within our organization before they even arise."

Time To Market
Complete Self-Assessment Guide

Notice of rights

Trademarks

Table of Contents

About The Art of Service

The Art of Service, Business Process Architects since 2000, is dedicated to helping stakeholders achieve excellence.

Defining, designing, creating, and implementing a process to solve a stakeholders challenge or meet an objective is the most valuable role... In EVERY group, company, organization and department.

Unless you're talking a one-time, single-use project, there should be a process. Whether that process is managed and implemented by humans, AI, or a combination of the two, it needs to be designed by someone with a complex enough perspective to ask the right questions.

Someone capable of asking the right questions and step back and say, 'What are we really trying to accomplish here? And is there a different way to look at it?'

With The Art of Service's Self-Assessments, we empower people who can do just that — whether their title is marketer, entrepreneur, manager, salesperson, consultant, Business Process Manager, executive assistant, IT Manager, CIO etc... —they are the people who rule the future. They are people who watch the process as it happens, and ask the right questions to make the process work better.

Contact us when you need any support with this Self-Assessment and any help with templates, blue-prints and examples of standard documents you might need:

https://theartofservice.com
support@theartofservice.com

Included Resources - how to access

Included with your purchase of the book is the Time To Market

Self-Assessment Spreadsheet Dashboard which contains all questions and Self-Assessment areas and auto-generates insights, graphs, and project RACI planning - all with examples to get you started right away.

How? Simply send an email to
access@theartofservice.com
with this books' title in the subject to get the Time To Market Self Assessment Tool right away.

The auto reply will guide you further, you will then receive the following contents with New and Updated specific criteria:

- The latest quick edition of the book in PDF
- The latest complete edition of the book in PDF, which criteria correspond to the criteria in...
- The Self-Assessment Excel Dashboard, and...
- Example pre-filled Self-Assessment Excel Dashboard to get familiar with results generation
- In-depth specific Checklists covering the topic
- Project management checklists and templates to assist with implementation

INCLUDES LIFETIME SELF ASSESSMENT UPDATES

Every self assessment comes with Lifetime Updates and Lifetime Free Updated Books. Lifetime Updates is an industry-first feature which allows you to receive verified self assessment updates, ensuring you always have the most accurate information at your fingertips.

Get it now- you will be glad you did - do it now, before you forget.

Send an email to **access@theartofservice.com** with this books' title in the subject to get the Time To Market Self Assessment Tool right away.

Purpose of this Self-Assessment

This Self-Assessment has been developed to improve understanding of the requirements and elements of Time To Market, based on best practices and standards in business process architecture, design and quality management.

It is designed to allow for a rapid Self-Assessment to determine how closely existing management practices and procedures correspond to the elements of the Self-Assessment.

The criteria of requirements and elements of Time To Market have been rephrased in the format of a Self-Assessment questionnaire, with a seven-criterion scoring system, as explained in this document.

In this format, even with limited background knowledge of Time To Market, a manager can quickly review existing operations to determine how they measure up to the standards. This in turn can serve as the starting point of a 'gap analysis' to identify management tools or system elements that might usefully be implemented in the organization to help improve overall performance.

How to use the Self-Assessment

On the following pages are a series of questions to identify to what extent your Time To Market initiative is complete in comparison to the requirements set in standards.

To facilitate answering the questions, there is a space in front of each question to enter a score on a scale of '1' to '5'.

1 Strongly Disagree

2 Disagree

3 Neutral

4 Agree

5 Strongly Agree

Read the question and rate it with the following in front of mind:

'In my belief, the answer to this question is clearly defined'.

There are two ways in which you can choose to interpret this statement;

1. how aware are you that the answer to the question is clearly defined
2. for more in-depth analysis you can choose to gather evidence and confirm the answer to the question. This obviously will take more time, most Self-Assessment users opt for the first way to interpret the question and dig deeper later on based on the outcome of the overall Self-Assessment.

A score of '1' would mean that the answer is not clear at all, where a '5' would mean the answer is crystal clear and defined. Leave emtpy when the question is not applicable or you don't want to answer it, you can skip it without affecting your score. Write your score in the space provided.

After you have responded to all the appropriate statements in each section, compute your average score for that section, using the formula provided, and round to the nearest tenth. Then transfer to the corresponding spoke in the Time To Market Scorecard on the second next page of the Self-Assessment.

Your completed Time To Market Scorecard will give you a clear presentation of which Time To Market areas need attention.

Time To Market Scorecard Example

Example of how the finalized Scorecard can look like:

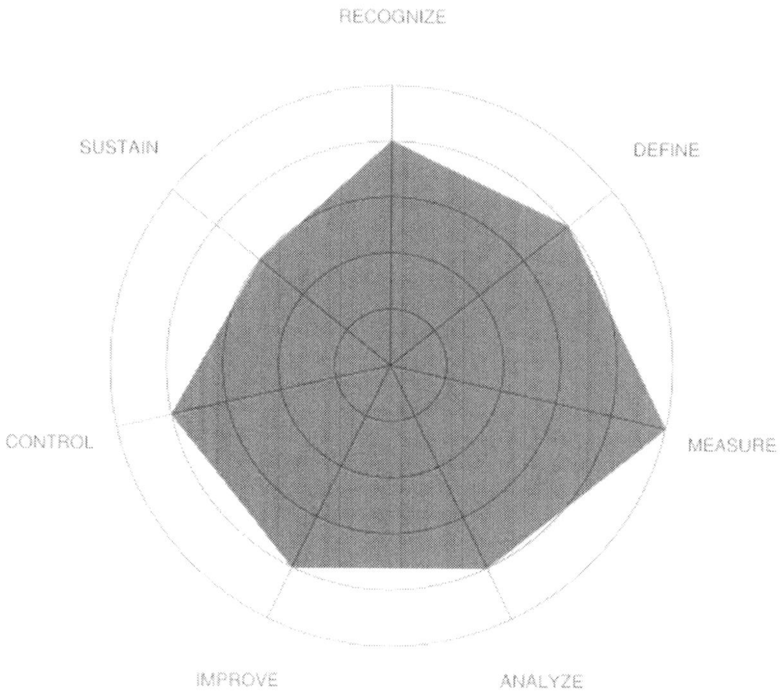

Time To Market Scorecard

Your Scores:

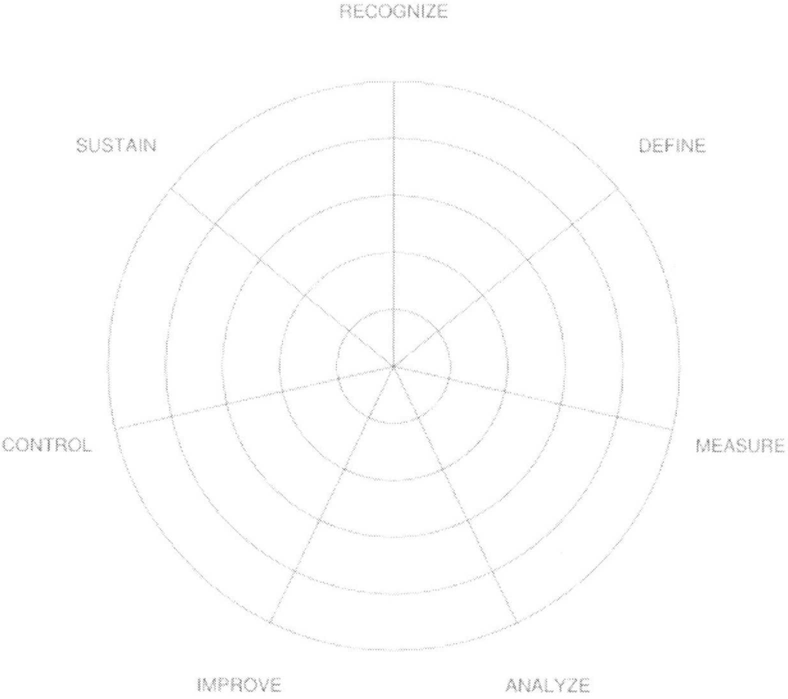

BEGINNING OF THE SELF-ASSESSMENT:

CRITERION #1: RECOGNIZE

INTENT: Be aware of the need for change. Recognize that there is an unfavorable variation, problem or symptom.

In my belief, the answer to this question is clearly defined:

5 Strongly Agree

4 Agree

3 Neutral

2 Disagree

1 Strongly Disagree

1. Where is training needed?
<--- Score

2. When is the best time to hold the event?
<--- Score

3. How do you recognize an Time to Market objection?
<--- Score

4. What extra resources will you need?
<--- Score

5. Who needs to know?
<--- Score

6. Why lose valuable time-to-market investigating a bug in your design if someone has already asked you about the same issue?
<--- Score

7. Do you need to avoid or amend any Time to Market activities?
<--- Score

8. Is there increasing recognition that agility is an imperative for success of your organization as it faces intense rivalry, globalization, and time to market pressures?
<--- Score

9. Does your organization need more Time to Market education?
<--- Score

10. How much time does the senior executive team give to marketing issues?
<--- Score

11. What resources or support might you need?
<--- Score

12. What creative shifts do you need to take?
<--- Score

13. Has a specific market segment been identified

and potential for commercialization examined?
<--- Score

14. Can management personnel recognize the monetary benefit of Time to Market?
<--- Score

15. Who needs to know about Time to Market?
<--- Score

16. What do you need to think about before investing loads of time in social media?
<--- Score

17. Are problem definition and motivation clearly presented?
<--- Score

18. Are there regulatory / compliance issues?
<--- Score

19. Which needs are not included or involved?
<--- Score

20. Has your organization identified how it will secure/acquire the necessary capacity over time to deliver the products or services to the customers?
<--- Score

21. What are the stakeholder objectives to be achieved with Time to Market?
<--- Score

22. How does it fit into your organizational needs and tasks?
<--- Score

23. What does Time to Market success mean to the stakeholders?
<--- Score

24. Do you need to run your business full-time?
<--- Score

25. What are the timeframes required to resolve each of the issues/problems?
<--- Score

26. Is it clear when you think of the day ahead of you what activities and tasks you need to complete?
<--- Score

27. Is there anything that will prevent you from getting to work on time?
<--- Score

28. What would happen if Time to Market weren't done?
<--- Score

29. Consider your own Time to Market project, what types of organizational problems do you think might be causing or affecting your problem, based on the work done so far?
<--- Score

30. Are there Time to Market problems defined?
<--- Score

31. What needs to stay?
<--- Score

32. How much time will participants need to commit to the program?
<--- Score

33. Who should resolve the Time to Market issues?
<--- Score

34. How are the Time to Market's objectives aligned to the group's overall stakeholder strategy?
<--- Score

35. Act/Adjust: What Do you Need to Do Differently?
<--- Score

36. What situation(s) led to this Time to Market Self Assessment?
<--- Score

37. Why is this needed?
<--- Score

38. What should be considered when identifying available resources, constraints, and deadlines?
<--- Score

39. What vendors make products that address the Time to Market needs?
<--- Score

40. What is needed for fastest time to market success?
<--- Score

41. How much are sponsors, customers, partners, stakeholders involved in Time to Market? In other words, what are the risks, if Time to Market does not

deliver successfully?
<--- Score

42. What are the expected benefits of Time to Market to the stakeholder?
<--- Score

43. Who else hopes to benefit from it?
<--- Score

44. Would you recognize a threat from the inside?
<--- Score

45. Has a specific market segment been identified?
<--- Score

46. What is the timing when do you need to act and over what time period?
<--- Score

47. What Time to Market problem should be solved?
<--- Score

48. Think about the people you identified for your Time to Market project and the project responsibilities you would assign to them, what kind of training do you think they would need to perform these responsibilities effectively?
<--- Score

49. What problems are you facing and how do you consider Time to Market will circumvent those obstacles?
<--- Score

50. How are you going to measure success?

<--- Score

51. What Time to Market coordination do you need?
<--- Score

52. As a sponsor, customer or management, how important is it to meet goals, objectives?
<--- Score

53. What time do you need to arrive?
<--- Score

54. Will it solve real problems?
<--- Score

55. What day/time do you prefer to attend an event?
<--- Score

56. Are there any specific expectations or concerns about the Time to Market team, Time to Market itself?
<--- Score

Add up total points for this section:
_____ = Total points for this section

Divided by: ______ (number of statements answered) = ______
Average score for this section

Transfer your score to the Time to Market Index at the beginning of the Self-Assessment.

CRITERION #2: DEFINE:

INTENT: Formulate the stakeholder problem. Define the problem, needs and objectives.

In my belief, the answer to this question is clearly defined:

5 Strongly Agree

4 Agree

3 Neutral

2 Disagree

1 Strongly Disagree

1. Has anyone else (internal or external to the group) attempted to solve this problem or a similar one before? If so, what knowledge can be leveraged from these previous efforts?
<--- Score

2. Has the improvement team collected the 'voice of the customer' (obtained feedback – qualitative and quantitative)?

<--- Score

3. How much time should your designated guerrilla spend attending to actions required by guerrilla marketing?
<--- Score

4. Is there a Time to Market management charter, including stakeholder case, problem and goal statements, scope, milestones, roles and responsibilities, communication plan?
<--- Score

5. What knowledge or experience is required?
<--- Score

6. How do you manage scope?
<--- Score

7. What gets examined?
<--- Score

8. Is the team formed and are team leaders (Coaches and Management Leads) assigned?
<--- Score

9. When are meeting minutes sent out? Who is on the distribution list?
<--- Score

10. Who are the Time to Market improvement team members, including Management Leads and Coaches?
<--- Score

11. Has everyone on the team, including the team

leaders, been properly trained?
<--- Score

12. Has the Time to Market work been fairly and/or equitably divided and delegated among team members who are qualified and capable to perform the work? Has everyone contributed?
<--- Score

13. Are the product requirements stable to support time to market of the product?
<--- Score

14. When is/was the Time to Market start date?
<--- Score

15. Are stakeholder processes mapped?
<--- Score

16. Is the team adequately staffed with the desired cross-functionality? If not, what additional resources are available to the team?
<--- Score

17. What time period is usually required to collect payments from customers?
<--- Score

18. Is the team sponsored by a champion or stakeholder leader?
<--- Score

19. Has a team charter been developed and communicated?
<--- Score

20. Has a project plan, Gantt chart, or similar been developed/completed?
<--- Score

21. Are improvement team members fully trained on Time to Market?
<--- Score

22. Have all basic functions of Time to Market been defined?
<--- Score

23. What is the scope of Time to Market?
<--- Score

24. Is the Time to Market scope complete and appropriately sized?
<--- Score

25. How was the 'as is' process map developed, reviewed, verified and validated?
<--- Score

26. How do you define time-to-market?
<--- Score

27. Have you considered if any new requirements from the customer or for the product?
<--- Score

28. How do you build the right business case?
<--- Score

29. Will team members regularly document their Time to Market work?
<--- Score

30. Are relevant market intermediaries required to maintain records that capital levels can be readily determined at any time?
<--- Score

31. Are customers identified and high impact areas defined?
<--- Score

32. What constraints exist that might impact the team?
<--- Score

33. How do you gather Time to Market requirements?
<--- Score

34. What is in the scope and what is not in scope?
<--- Score

35. Has the direction changed at all during the course of Time to Market? If so, when did it change and why?
<--- Score

36. What is the worst case scenario?
<--- Score

37. Do the problem and goal statements meet the SMART criteria (specific, measurable, attainable, relevant, and time-bound)?
<--- Score

38. How and when will the baselines be defined?
<--- Score

39. Is the Time to Market scope manageable?

<--- Score

40. What are the compelling stakeholder reasons for embarking on Time to Market?
<--- Score

41. How do you define time to market?
<--- Score

42. Is Time to Market currently on schedule according to the plan?
<--- Score

43. What system do you use for gathering Time to Market information?
<--- Score

44. What key stakeholder process output measure(s) does Time to Market leverage and how?
<--- Score

45. Is the improvement team aware of the different versions of a process: what they think it is vs. what it actually is vs. what it should be vs. what it could be?
<--- Score

46. What is out-of-scope initially?
<--- Score

47. When is the estimated completion date?
<--- Score

48. How will variation in the actual durations of each activity be dealt with to ensure that the expected Time to Market results are met?
<--- Score

49. Is the scope of Time to Market defined?
<--- Score

50. How much time and other resources will be required to market the program?
<--- Score

51. Will team members perform Time to Market work when assigned and in a timely fashion?
<--- Score

52. If substitutes have been appointed, have they been briefed on the Time to Market goals and received regular communications as to the progress to date?
<--- Score

53. What is the context?
<--- Score

54. How have you defined all Time to Market requirements first?
<--- Score

55. How will the Time to Market team and the group measure complete success of Time to Market?
<--- Score

56. Do you all define Time to Market in the same way?
<--- Score

57. Is there a completed SIPOC representation, describing the Suppliers, Inputs, Process, Outputs, and Customers?
<--- Score

58. Is there a requirement to spend time in the office?
<--- Score

59. What would be the goal or target for a Time to Market's improvement team?
<--- Score

60. What sort of initial information to gather?
<--- Score

61. Are there different segments of customers?
<--- Score

62. How much time should your designated Guerrilla spend attending to the actions required by Guerrilla Marketing?
<--- Score

63. Is a fully trained team formed, supported, and committed to work on the Time to Market improvements?
<--- Score

64. Who is gathering Time to Market information?
<--- Score

65. What are (control) requirements for Time to Market Information?
<--- Score

66. Are there any constraints known that bear on the ability to perform Time to Market work? How is the team addressing them?
<--- Score

67. Are customer(s) identified and segmented according to their different needs and requirements?
<--- Score

68. What scope do you want your strategy to cover?
<--- Score

69. Is there a critical path to deliver Time to Market results?
<--- Score

70. Has/have the customer(s) been identified?
<--- Score

71. What are the dynamics of the communication plan?
<--- Score

72. Is full participation by members in regularly held team meetings guaranteed?
<--- Score

73. Does the team have regular meetings?
<--- Score

74. Are you dedicated or able to spend the time required to meet market obligations?
<--- Score

75. What is the scope of the Time to Market work?
<--- Score

76. What specifically is the problem? Where does it occur? When does it occur? What is its extent?
<--- Score

77. What customer feedback methods were used to solicit their input?
<--- Score

78. How do you gather requirements?
<--- Score

79. Is there a completed, verified, and validated high-level 'as is' (not 'should be' or 'could be') stakeholder process map?
<--- Score

80. Is Time to Market linked to key stakeholder goals and objectives?
<--- Score

81. What time frame do you require the approval to be confirmed or rejected?
<--- Score

82. What are the Roles and Responsibilities for each team member and its leadership? Where is this documented?
<--- Score

83. Is it clearly defined in and to your organization what you do?
<--- Score

84. How do you keep key subject matter experts in the loop?
<--- Score

85. Which service platform will be the appropriate one to satisfy the requirements for innovative

services and short time to market?
<--- Score

86. Are different versions of process maps needed to account for the different types of inputs?
<--- Score

87. Is the team equipped with available and reliable resources?
<--- Score

88. How does the Time to Market manager ensure against scope creep?
<--- Score

89. Is the current 'as is' process being followed? If not, what are the discrepancies?
<--- Score

90. Is there regularly 100% attendance at the team meetings? If not, have appointed substitutes attended to preserve cross-functionality and full representation?
<--- Score

91. How do you catch Time to Market definition inconsistencies?
<--- Score

92. Has a high-level 'as is' process map been completed, verified and validated?
<--- Score

93. How did the Time to Market manager receive input to the development of a Time to Market improvement plan and the estimated completion

dates/times of each activity?
<--- Score

94. Are team charters developed?
<--- Score

95. Have specific policy objectives been defined?
<--- Score

96. How is the team tracking and documenting its work?
<--- Score

97. Are audit criteria, scope, frequency and methods defined?
<--- Score

98. What are the rough order estimates on cost savings/opportunities that Time to Market brings?
<--- Score

99. Are accountability and ownership for Time to Market clearly defined?
<--- Score

100. Are approval levels defined for contracts and supplements to contracts?
<--- Score

101. Are you struggling to define the role of product marketing?
<--- Score

102. How do you manage unclear Time to Market requirements?
<--- Score

103. Do you accept that building a strong market for your work requires time and cooperation?
<--- Score

104. Is the work to date meeting requirements?
<--- Score

105. Have the customer needs been translated into specific, measurable requirements? How?
<--- Score

106. What are the boundaries of the scope? What is in bounds and what is not? What is the start point? What is the stop point?
<--- Score

107. What critical content must be communicated – who, what, when, where, and how?
<--- Score

108. Is data collected and displayed to better understand customer(s) critical needs and requirements.
<--- Score

109. How often are the team meetings?
<--- Score

110. The political context: who holds power?
<--- Score

Add up total points for this section:
_____ = Total points for this section

Divided by: ______ (number of

statements answered) = ______
Average score for this section

Transfer your score to the Time to Market Index at the beginning of the Self-Assessment.

CRITERION #3: MEASURE:

INTENT: Gather the correct data. Measure the current performance and evolution of the situation.

In my belief, the answer to this question is clearly defined:

5 Strongly Agree

4 Agree

3 Neutral

2 Disagree

1 Strongly Disagree

1. What key measures identified indicate the performance of the stakeholder process?
<--- Score

2. What are hidden Time to Market quality costs?
<--- Score

3. What experiences can be found on the market and when is the right time to begin the detailed

analysis?
<--- Score

4. Which Time to Market impacts are significant?
<--- Score

5. What causes investor action?
<--- Score

6. What are the Time to Market key cost drivers?
<--- Score

7. What are allowable costs?
<--- Score

8. How frequently do you track Time to Market measures?
<--- Score

9. How does integration relate to system performance, time-to-market and cost?
<--- Score

10. Are the measurements objective?
<--- Score

11. Is there a Performance Baseline?
<--- Score

12. When is it time to look beyond your initial market – and what should you prioritize when the time comes?
<--- Score

13. How do your measurements capture actionable Time to Market information for use in exceeding your

customers expectations and securing your customers engagement?
<--- Score

14. What can be done to reduce the high costs which result from the long driving time?
<--- Score

15. How frequently do you verify your Time to Market strategy?
<--- Score

16. How do you quantify and qualify impacts?
<--- Score

17. Is long term and short term variability accounted for?
<--- Score

18. How to cause the change?
<--- Score

19. Are the units of measure consistent?
<--- Score

20. Do you aggressively reward and promote the people who have the biggest impact on creating excellent Time to Market services/products?
<--- Score

21. Why is the promise of COTS (commercial off the shelf) applications – reduced time to market and IT costs via ready-made functionality – tainted by upgrade headaches?
<--- Score

22. What is your decision requirements diagram?
<--- Score

23. How can you reduce costs?
<--- Score

24. How do you balance time-to-market, agility, quality, and cost?
<--- Score

25. Why a Time to Market focus?
<--- Score

26. Was a life-cycle cost analysis performed?
<--- Score

27. What are predictive Time to Market analytics?
<--- Score

28. Has a specific market segment been clearly identified and quantified?
<--- Score

29. What is the cost of rework?
<--- Score

30. How will measures be used to manage and adapt?
<--- Score

31. How do you focus on what is right -not who is right?
<--- Score

32. Is data collected on key measures that were identified?
<--- Score

33. Is it limited to a small number of domains, a specific real-time block list (RBL), or a general issue impacting delivery across your entire email program?
<--- Score

34. Have you found any 'ground fruit' or 'low-hanging fruit' for immediate remedies to the gap in performance?
<--- Score

35. What are the agreed upon definitions of the high impact areas, defect(s), unit(s), and opportunities that will figure into the process capability metrics?
<--- Score

36. Which top level product metrics namely quality, cost and time to market conflicted most with the commonality strategy chosen?
<--- Score

37. What causes slow time to markets?
<--- Score

38. What disadvantage does this cause for the user?
<--- Score

39. What is your cost benefit analysis?
<--- Score

40. Who should receive measurement reports?
<--- Score

41. What users will be impacted?
<--- Score

42. When is Root Cause Analysis Required?
<--- Score

43. Do the benefits outweigh the costs?
<--- Score

44. How sensitive must the Time to Market strategy be to cost?
<--- Score

45. Where is it measured?
<--- Score

46. How are you verifying it?
<--- Score

47. Are missed Time to Market opportunities costing your organization money?
<--- Score

48. Are supply costs steady or fluctuating?
<--- Score

49. What causes extra work or rework?
<--- Score

50. Are high impact defects defined and identified in the stakeholder process?
<--- Score

51. Are process variation components displayed/ communicated using suitable charts, graphs, plots?
<--- Score

52. How much does it cost (in time and resources)

to acquire a customer?
<--- Score

53. How was commonality linked to the top level metrics of the product namely quality, cost and time to market?
<--- Score

54. Can the design of the part be simplified to reduce its basic cost?
<--- Score

55. Is your time to market adversely impacted by a disjointed decision making process?
<--- Score

56. How will you measure your Time to Market effectiveness?
<--- Score

57. Is the cost worth the Time to Market effort ?
<--- Score

58. What is an unallowable cost?
<--- Score

59. What measurements are being captured?
<--- Score

60. Is a follow-up focused external Time to Market review required?
<--- Score

61. Are Time to Market vulnerabilities categorized and prioritized?
<--- Score

62. Do you look for vendors whose solutions are designed to facilitate your objectives. Do solutions promote efficiencies, reduce costs, mitigate compliance related risks and speed time to market?
<--- Score

63. Are you under pressure to provide always-on IT, faster time to market, and reduce costs?
<--- Score

64. How much time and how many people do you have to carry out analysis?
<--- Score

65. What are the Time to Market investment costs?
<--- Score

66. How do you achieve growth, shorten the time-to-market and reduce the cost of failure?
<--- Score

67. What is the total cost related to deploying Time to Market, including any consulting or professional services?
<--- Score

68. How will the Time to Market data be analyzed?
<--- Score

69. What charts has the team used to display the components of variation in the process?
<--- Score

70. What happens if cost savings do not materialize?

<--- Score

71. At what cost?
<--- Score

72. Have the concerns of stakeholders to help identify and define potential barriers been obtained and analyzed?
<--- Score

73. Are suppliers contributing suggestions to reduce cost?
<--- Score

74. How are real–time consumer conversations impacting marketing decision–making?
<--- Score

75. Do solutions promote efficiencies, reduce costs, mitigate compliance-related risks and speed time to market?
<--- Score

76. How does you balance time to market, cost concerns, security, manageability and risk in the move to a cloud-connected enterprise?
<--- Score

77. Is key measure data collection planned and executed, process variation displayed and communicated and performance baselined?
<--- Score

78. How do you balance time to market, agility, quality, and cost?
<--- Score

79. What does a Test Case verify?
<--- Score

80. How do you verify the Time to Market requirements quality?
<--- Score

81. Is Process Variation Displayed/Communicated?
<--- Score

82. How long to keep data and how to manage retention costs?
<--- Score

83. How large is the gap between current performance and the customer-specified (goal) performance?
<--- Score

84. When a disaster occurs, who gets priority?
<--- Score

85. What is the real cost, including opportunity cost in time to market?
<--- Score

86. How do you control the overall costs of your work processes?
<--- Score

87. Does management have the right priorities among projects?
<--- Score

88. What determines where to focus your time and

resources on Social Media?
<--- Score

89. Was a business case (cost/benefit) developed?
<--- Score

90. What data was collected (past, present, future/ ongoing)?
<--- Score

91. Is the measure of success for Time to Market understandable to a variety of people?
<--- Score

92. Do you have a flow diagram of what happens?
<--- Score

93. What would be a real cause for concern?
<--- Score

94. What could cause you to change course?
<--- Score

95. Did you tackle the cause or the symptom?
<--- Score

96. How do you satisfy elevated quality expectations while accelerating your time to market and reducing costs?
<--- Score

97. What are the costs/benefits of time-to-market versus time-to-market acceptance?
<--- Score

98. Are you spending enough time meeting

analysts face-to-face?
<--- Score

99. How do you verify performance?
<--- Score

100. What is the impact on time to market?
<--- Score

101. What particular quality tools did the team find helpful in establishing measurements?
<--- Score

102. What are the costs?
<--- Score

103. What have you done to reduce your departments operational costs or to save time?
<--- Score

104. Are key measures identified and agreed upon?
<--- Score

105. How do you measure segment stability over time?
<--- Score

106. What could cause delays in the schedule?
<--- Score

107. Is a solid data collection plan established that includes measurement systems analysis?
<--- Score

108. How to measure segment stability over time?
<--- Score

109. What has the team done to assure the stability and accuracy of the measurement process?
<--- Score

110. What is the Time to Market business impact?
<--- Score

111. Will you have to train people, and at what cost (money, time)?
<--- Score

112. What are the key input variables? What are the key process variables? What are the key output variables?
<--- Score

113. How does cost-to-serve analysis help?
<--- Score

114. What impact does the current testing needs have on time to market?
<--- Score

115. How do the leaders reduce costs while also reducing time to market and enabling innovation?
<--- Score

116. Is your project ready for time to market focus?
<--- Score

117. Who participated in the data collection for measurements?
<--- Score

118. Are you continually being asked to reduce

costs, decrease time to market and improve inventory velocity?
<--- Score

119. Is data collection planned and executed?
<--- Score

120. How to reduce costs and time to market associated with new or changed policies?
<--- Score

121. Was a data collection plan established?
<--- Score

Add up total points for this section:
_____ = Total points for this section

Divided by: ______ (number of statements answered) = ______ Average score for this section

Transfer your score to the Time to Market Index at the beginning of the Self-Assessment.

CRITERION #4: ANALYZE:

INTENT: Analyze causes, assumptions and hypotheses.

In my belief, the answer to this question is clearly defined:

5 Strongly Agree

4 Agree

3 Neutral

2 Disagree

1 Strongly Disagree

1. Are you willing to make daily deliveries and timely deliveries, and offer special varieties, freshness, personal attention and a quick response to any problems that arise?
<--- Score

2. Did any value-added analysis or 'lean thinking' take place to identify some of the gaps shown on the 'as is' process map?
<--- Score

3. Do your contracts/agreements contain data security obligations?
<--- Score

4. What were the crucial 'moments of truth' on the process map?
<--- Score

5. Is the access to data aimed at developing new products or improving existing products?
<--- Score

6. Is there any way to speed up the process?
<--- Score

7. Who will gather what data?
<--- Score

8. What is your organizations process which leads to recognition of value generation?
<--- Score

9. How will the Time to Market data be captured?
<--- Score

10. What are the Time to Market design outputs?
<--- Score

11. Were Pareto charts (or similar) used to portray the 'heavy hitters' (or key sources of variation)?
<--- Score

12. Do the systems process and produce information in an efficient, timely manner?
<--- Score

13. How will the data be checked for quality?
<--- Score

14. When looking at the timeframes for innovation processes and time to market?
<--- Score

15. Record-keeping requirements flow from the records needed as inputs, outputs, controls and for transformation of a Time to Market process, are the records needed as inputs to the Time to Market process available?
<--- Score

16. Is the Time to Market process severely broken such that a re-design is necessary?
<--- Score

17. How many times are you allowed to use the data?
<--- Score

18. How does a superior machine automation system contribute to quicker build times?
<--- Score

19. How do other organizations begin and justify data quality improvements?
<--- Score

20. Did any additional data need to be collected?
<--- Score

21. Do staff qualifications match your project?
<--- Score

22. What quality tools were used to get through the analyze phase?
<--- Score

23. What Time to Market data should be collected?
<--- Score

24. Will adoption of Cloud technology enable quicker time to market than an on premise deployment?
<--- Score

25. What are the processes for audit reporting and management?
<--- Score

26. How do you identify specific Time to Market investment opportunities and emerging trends?
<--- Score

27. What are the revised rough estimates of the financial savings/opportunity for Time to Market improvements?
<--- Score

28. How much time did it take to complete the process?
<--- Score

29. Which is more relevant to marketing historical or real time data?
<--- Score

30. What tools were used to narrow the list of possible causes?

<--- Score

31. How do you make the right decision with regards to process changes and harmonization to create a balance between functionality and time to market?
<--- Score

32. Who will facilitate the team and process?
<--- Score

33. How you can use technology to accelerate time to market quicker and more effectively?
<--- Score

34. What tools were used to generate the list of possible causes?
<--- Score

35. How was the detailed process map generated, verified, and validated?
<--- Score

36. How do you deliver insights to the right people at the right time to act on and react to opportunities and threats in the marketplace?
<--- Score

37. What is the total processing time?
<--- Score

38. What does the data say about the performance of the stakeholder process?
<--- Score

39. What is the basic use of a prototype during the

new product development process?
<--- Score

40. Are there sources of data which can inform new product development?
<--- Score

41. How will corresponding data be collected?
<--- Score

42. What Time to Market data should be managed?
<--- Score

43. What process does the developer follow to make sure projects are completed on time and on budget?
<--- Score

44. How can organizations conduct business processes overhaul to reduce time to market while remaining competitive in terms of product variety and price?
<--- Score

45. Do you use data to develop products and services in adjacent or new business sectors?
<--- Score

46. Where is the data coming from to measure compliance?
<--- Score

47. What is the cost of poor quality as supported by the team's analysis?
<--- Score

48. Have you defined which data is gathered how?
<--- Score

49. Are gaps between current performance and the goal performance identified?
<--- Score

50. Did you define minimum and maximum latency prior to the purchase of the real-time speed data?
<--- Score

51. What conclusions were drawn from the team's data collection and analysis? How did the team reach these conclusions?
<--- Score

52. Is the performance gap determined?
<--- Score

53. What Time to Market data will be collected?
<--- Score

54. What were the financial benefits resulting from any 'ground fruit or low-hanging fruit' (quick fixes)?
<--- Score

55. How do you ensure that the Time to Market opportunity is realistic?
<--- Score

56. Did you feel the database and the server were accessible every time the App tried to POST/GET?
<--- Score

57. Were any designed experiments used to generate

additional insight into the data analysis?
<--- Score

58. Are you missing Time to Market opportunities?
<--- Score

59. Think about the functions involved in your Time to Market project, what processes flow from these functions?
<--- Score

60. Is the final output clearly identified?
<--- Score

61. Is the required Time to Market data gathered?
<--- Score

62. Has an output goal been set?
<--- Score

63. What qualifications do Time to Market leaders need?
<--- Score

64. Do quality systems drive continuous improvement?
<--- Score

65. Have the problem and goal statements been updated to reflect the additional knowledge gained from the analyze phase?
<--- Score

66. What systems/processes must you excel at?
<--- Score

67. Have any additional benefits been identified that will result from closing all or most of the gaps?
<--- Score

68. How often will data be collected for measures?
<--- Score

69. Is the suppliers process defined and controlled?
<--- Score

70. What did the team gain from developing a sub-process map?
<--- Score

71. Has your organization built up a database on clients from intake to exit?
<--- Score

72. Were there any improvement opportunities identified from the process analysis?
<--- Score

73. Was a cause-and-effect diagram used to explore the different types of causes (or sources of variation)?
<--- Score

74. What are your current levels and trends in key Time to Market measures or indicators of product and process performance that are important to and directly serve your customers?
<--- Score

75. What output to create?
<--- Score

76. What are your outputs?

<--- Score

77. What training and qualifications will you need?
<--- Score

78. Is the gap/opportunity displayed and communicated in financial terms?
<--- Score

79. Does the system have an integrated (real-time) eCommerce site tied to the ticketing database?
<--- Score

80. What better time to market than when someone is in the process of buying already?
<--- Score

81. Is data and process analysis, root cause analysis and quantifying the gap/opportunity in place?
<--- Score

82. Was a detailed process map created to amplify critical steps of the 'as is' stakeholder process?
<--- Score

83. How much data can be collected in the given timeframe?
<--- Score

84. Is there an established change management process?
<--- Score

85. How is data used for program management and improvement?
<--- Score

86. What are your current levels and trends in key measures or indicators of Time to Market product and process performance that are important to and directly serve your customers? How do these results compare with the performance of your competitors and other organizations with similar offerings?
<--- Score

87. What are evaluation criteria for the output?
<--- Score

88. When should a process be art not science?
<--- Score

89. How do you reduce time to market without sacrificing product or data quality?
<--- Score

90. What is the output?
<--- Score

91. What is the oversight process?
<--- Score

92. What qualifies as competition?
<--- Score

93. Has your organization built up a database on its clients from intake to exit?
<--- Score

Add up total points for this section:
_____ = Total points for this section

Divided by: ______ (number of

statements answered) = ______
Average score for this section

Transfer your score to the Time to Market Index at the beginning of the Self-Assessment.

CRITERION #5: IMPROVE:

INTENT: Develop a practical solution. Innovate, establish and test the solution and to measure the results.

In my belief, the answer to this question is clearly defined:

5 Strongly Agree

4 Agree

3 Neutral

2 Disagree

1 Strongly Disagree

1. What is the degree/intensity of new product development, in general, in your organization?
<--- Score

2. Are new and improved process ('should be') maps developed?
<--- Score

3. Who are the Time to Market decision makers?

<--- Score

4. How do you improve Time to Market service perception, and satisfaction?
<--- Score

5. How to speed up time to market to enable early market deployment of new solutions with?
<--- Score

6. Does the solution accelerate your time to market?
<--- Score

7. How are time to markets being improved?
<--- Score

8. Does a good decision guarantee a good outcome?
<--- Score

9. Is there a cost/benefit analysis of optimal solution(s)?
<--- Score

10. Are risk management tasks balanced centrally and locally?
<--- Score

11. Does senior management view a flexible IT infrastructure as providing a competitive advantage by enabling new initiatives, efficiencies and improved time to market?
<--- Score

12. How is the real-time payments market continuing to develop?

<--- Score

13. What measure do you use most commonly to evaluate your timeliness in moving products to market?
<--- Score

14. What are the main reasons for using modular New Product Development within organization A?
<--- Score

15. What challenges does your organization face in developing and introducing new products?
<--- Score

16. How does your organization meet the increasing regulatory compliance demands while improving product quality and decreasing time to market for new products?
<--- Score

17. How can the phases of Time to Market development be identified?
<--- Score

18. Does evaluation system apply to new product development and significant projects as well as to continuous operations?
<--- Score

19. What are the business benefits of using the new development or function for the customer?
<--- Score

20. What tools were most useful during the improve phase?

<--- Score

21. Which is the cloud characteristics that speeds up development, deployment, and overall time to market?
<--- Score

22. What is the overall quality, risk, time to market and value of your services?
<--- Score

23. How to substantially reduce the vehicle development lead-time and meet required time to market with consistent or improved quality and similar or reduced investments?
<--- Score

24. What is the time interval after the successful completion of the project to evaluate what went right and wrong?
<--- Score

25. Are you willing to invest the time and money to develop a website for your business?
<--- Score

26. How could a cloud computing based development platform speed time to market?
<--- Score

27. How do you improve productivity?
<--- Score

28. What lessons, if any, from a pilot were incorporated into the design of the full-scale solution?
<--- Score

29. Is there a time to market improvement compared to last year?
<--- Score

30. What do you need to optimize for the next time?
<--- Score

31. Is a contingency plan established?
<--- Score

32. How fast can developers provision a server to host a new application in production?
<--- Score

33. Do you cover the five essential competencies: Communication, Collaboration,Innovation, Adaptability, and Leadership that improve an organizations ability to leverage the new Time to Market in a volatile global economy?
<--- Score

34. Describe the design of the pilot and what tests were conducted, if any?
<--- Score

35. Can an API improve operational efficiency and decrease time to market?
<--- Score

36. What might a manufacturer and a customer consider about the pricing of a newly developed product?
<--- Score

37. What are new products you can develop?
<--- Score

38. How to optimize campaigns at the time of creation?
<--- Score

39. Are you developing new product to launch in international market?
<--- Score

40. Do vendor agreements bring new compliance risk ?
<--- Score

41. What alternative responses are available to manage risk?
<--- Score

42. How will the group know that the solution worked?
<--- Score

43. How can skill-level changes improve Time to Market?
<--- Score

44. How are policy decisions made and where?
<--- Score

45. Are the key business and technology risks being managed?
<--- Score

46. How do you measure progress and evaluate training effectiveness?

<--- Score

47. Are you assessing Time to Market and risk?
<--- Score

48. How do you mitigate Time to Market risk?
<--- Score

49. How can marketers capture context in real time and develop insights to predict consumer behaviour?
<--- Score

50. Are possible solutions generated and tested?
<--- Score

51. What error proofing will be done to address some of the discrepancies observed in the 'as is' process?
<--- Score

52. Are your competitors investing in the development of new products with positive social and environmental attributes?
<--- Score

53. Who are the Time to Market decision-makers?
<--- Score

54. Is there any other Time to Market solution?
<--- Score

55. What were the criteria for evaluating a Time to Market pilot?
<--- Score

56. How do you increase the time to market and

reduce development time for new products?
<--- Score

57. For estimation problems, how do you develop an estimation statement?
<--- Score

58. What is the Time to Development?
<--- Score

59. How could a cloud computing -based development platform speed time to market?
<--- Score

60. What does the 'should be' process map/design look like?
<--- Score

61. Who will be using the results of the measurement activities?
<--- Score

62. How do you manage and improve your Time to Market work systems to deliver customer value and achieve organizational success and sustainability?
<--- Score

63. Will you have sufficient time to develop the product before its market value begins to decrease?
<--- Score

64. Is there a high likelihood that any recommendations will achieve their intended results?
<--- Score

65. Are the risks fully understood, reasonable and manageable?
<--- Score

66. What assumptions are made about the solution and approach?
<--- Score

67. Who do you seek information from when developing new products?
<--- Score

68. Who makes the Time to Market decisions in your organization?
<--- Score

69. What is new product development?
<--- Score

70. Was a pilot designed for the proposed solution(s)?
<--- Score

71. What communications are necessary to support the implementation of the solution?
<--- Score

72. How do you measure risk?
<--- Score

73. Are decisions made in a timely manner?
<--- Score

74. Is there sufficient time for partners to pilot and adopt the innovation within the project timeframe?
<--- Score

75. How to speed up Time to market to enable early market deployment of new solutions?
<--- Score

76. What attendant changes will need to be made to ensure that the solution is successful?
<--- Score

77. What actions can be taken to decrease time to internal market and development time of Cloud Infra-Services?
<--- Score

78. Is a cross-functional team involved in marketing decisions for a new product?
<--- Score

79. What tools were used to tap into the creativity and encourage 'outside the box' thinking?
<--- Score

80. How do you measure and improve competitive differentiators as time to market and price?
<--- Score

81. How can you improve Time to Market?
<--- Score

82. How does your organization evaluate strategic Time to Market success?
<--- Score

83. Will the project result in a time-to-market advantage over competition?
<--- Score

84. How is knowledge sharing about risk management improved?
<--- Score

85. Does it manage its raw materials and finished goods inventories in an optimal fashion according to just-in-time principles?
<--- Score

86. Is pilot data collected and analyzed?
<--- Score

87. What is the implementation plan?
<--- Score

88. Can you integrate quality management and risk management?
<--- Score

89. Have you achieved Time to Market improvements?
<--- Score

90. Who will be responsible for documenting the Time to Market requirements in detail?
<--- Score

91. Are there any constraints (technical, political, cultural, or otherwise) that would inhibit certain solutions?
<--- Score

92. When it comes time to sell something to your customer, what are the tools and tactics you use to make the decision to buy an easy one?
<--- Score

93. How fast is your time to resolution of alerts and incidents?
<--- Score

94. Where do you need Time to Market improvement?
<--- Score

95. What are the implications of the one critical Time to Market decision 10 minutes, 10 months, and 10 years from now?
<--- Score

96. What is Time to Market risk?
<--- Score

97. Who manages supplier risk management in your organization?
<--- Score

98. How to proceed when developing new products?
<--- Score

99. Is there a strong business demand to improve Time to Market?
<--- Score

100. How do you measure improved Time to Market service perception, and satisfaction?
<--- Score

101. Does your organization operate in an industry branch that includes development of new materials in product design?
<--- Score

102. Are the most efficient solutions problem-specific?
<--- Score

103. How should the application of new development models be supported from a cultural standpoint?
<--- Score

104. Has the purchasing strategy been assessed to ensure that COTS elements of the solution subject to rapid change in the marketplace are acquired using just-in-time principles?
<--- Score

105. Is your organization to develop products faster and accelerate time to market?
<--- Score

106. Do you work with users and early adopters to develop prototypes of new products and services?
<--- Score

107. How will the team or the process owner(s) monitor the implementation plan to see that it is working as intended?
<--- Score

108. Explorations of the frontiers of Time to Market will help you build influence, improve Time to Market, optimize decision making, and sustain change, what is your approach?
<--- Score

109. What organizational structures are used to manage new-product development?

<--- Score

110. Is there a small-scale pilot for proposed improvement(s)? What conclusions were drawn from the outcomes of a pilot?
<--- Score

111. How is continuous improvement applied to risk management?
<--- Score

112. How can companies improve time to market?
<--- Score

113. How did the team generate the list of possible solutions?
<--- Score

114. Who do you report Time to Market results to?
<--- Score

115. Are improved process ('should be') maps modified based on pilot data and analysis?
<--- Score

116. Is the implementation plan designed?
<--- Score

117. How will you know that you have improved?
<--- Score

118. Are the best solutions selected?
<--- Score

119. Can quality-oriented organizations develop innovative new products?

<--- Score

120. Were any criteria developed to assist the team in testing and evaluating potential solutions?
<--- Score

121. If time to market is an important element in the model, then : using that as a reference, what are the decision-makers trading off in the decision?
<--- Score

122. Which Time to Market solution is appropriate?
<--- Score

123. How do you improve your time to market?
<--- Score

124. Is the Time to Market solution sustainable?
<--- Score

125. Are procedures documented for managing Time to Market risks?
<--- Score

126. What are the Time to Market security risks?
<--- Score

127. What are the steps for new product development?
<--- Score

128. What were the underlying assumptions on the cost-benefit analysis?
<--- Score

129. Is time to market an important factor for your product development?
<--- Score

130. How risky is your organization?
<--- Score

131. If you could go back in time five years, what decision would you make differently? What is your best guess as to what decision you're making today you might regret five years from now?
<--- Score

132. Is a solution implementation plan established, including schedule/work breakdown structure, resources, risk management plan, cost/budget, and control plan?
<--- Score

133. How do you select the design solution that will be developed?
<--- Score

134. What is the team's contingency plan for potential problems occurring in implementation?
<--- Score

135. What tools were used to evaluate the potential solutions?
<--- Score

136. What is the improvement in time to receive information?
<--- Score

137. Is the optimal solution selected based on testing

and analysis?
<--- Score

138. How are Time to Market risks managed?
<--- Score

139. Do you have the optimal project management team structure?
<--- Score

140. Where do the Time to Market decisions reside?
<--- Score

141. Has the purchasing strategy been assessed to ensure that the COTS elements of the solution, which are subject to rapid change in the marketplace, are acquired using just-in-time principles?
<--- Score

142. How to find optimal time for sending an email?
<--- Score

143. What are the business benefits of using the new/changed development or function for the customer?
<--- Score

144. Do you favour time-to-market or evaluation accuracy?
<--- Score

145. How do you improve time to market?
<--- Score

146. How can a software development organization improve quality and speed time to market?
<--- Score

147. How has oCzs time to market improved since toshibas acquisition?
<--- Score

148. How does the solution remove the key sources of issues discovered in the analyze phase?
<--- Score

149. Do you test prototype solutions in one months time as opposed to a year?
<--- Score

150. Are business leaders looking for ways to improve organizational agility and time to market?
<--- Score

151. Is Time to Market documentation maintained?
<--- Score

152. What is Time to Market's impact on utilizing the best solution(s)?
<--- Score

Add up total points for this section:
_____ = Total points for this section

Divided by: ______ (number of statements answered) = ______
Average score for this section

Transfer your score to the Time to Market Index at the beginning of the Self-Assessment.

CRITERION #6: CONTROL:

INTENT: Implement the practical solution. Maintain the performance and correct possible complications.

In my belief, the answer to this question is clearly defined:

5 Strongly Agree

4 Agree

3 Neutral

2 Disagree

1 Strongly Disagree

1. What are the known security controls?
<--- Score

2. How are you doing compared to other vendors in your market in terms of on time, on standard delivery?
<--- Score

3. You may have created your quality measures at a

time when you lacked resources, technology wasn't up to the required standard, or low service levels were the industry norm. Have those circumstances changed?
<--- Score

4. What are your plans to decrease both planned and unplanned down time?
<--- Score

5. What standards does your organization use to provide real-time information via mobile devices?
<--- Score

6. What are the key elements of your Time to Market performance improvement system, including your evaluation, organizational learning, and innovation processes?
<--- Score

7. What key inputs and outputs are being measured on an ongoing basis?
<--- Score

8. Does a troubleshooting guide exist or is it needed?
<--- Score

9. Is new knowledge gained imbedded in the response plan?
<--- Score

10. Who is going to spread your message?
<--- Score

11. Has the improved process and its steps been standardized?

<--- Score

12. What should the next improvement project be that is related to Time to Market?
<--- Score

13. What is the physical space that must be represented to include all major factors, and what are the time scales that must be considered?
<--- Score

14. Is reporting being used or needed?
<--- Score

15. Are there documented procedures?
<--- Score

16. How will new or emerging customer needs/requirements be checked/communicated to orient the process toward meeting the new specifications and continually reducing variation?
<--- Score

17. What are the critical parameters to watch?
<--- Score

18. What do your reports reflect?
<--- Score

19. How do your controls stack up?
<--- Score

20. Does job training on the documented procedures need to be part of the process team's education and training?
<--- Score

21. What is the typical training time both to commence standard operation and to fully optimize the models?
<--- Score

22. Who has control over resources?
<--- Score

23. Does the response plan contain a definite closed loop continual improvement scheme (e.g., plan-do-check-act)?
<--- Score

24. Is the standard transaction fee charged to your organization each time a customer sends or receives funds?
<--- Score

25. Where do ideas that reach policy makers and planners as proposals for Time to Market strengthening and reform actually originate?
<--- Score

26. How will the day-to-day responsibilities for monitoring and continual improvement be transferred from the improvement team to the process owner?
<--- Score

27. Is a response plan established and deployed?
<--- Score

28. What do you need to do to build time management into your plan?
<--- Score

29. In the case of a Time to Market project, the criteria for the audit derive from implementation objectives, an audit of a Time to Market project involves assessing whether the recommendations outlined for implementation have been met, can you track that any Time to Market project is implemented as planned, and is it working?
<--- Score

30. How will the process owner and team be able to hold the gains?
<--- Score

31. Is there a recommended audit plan for routine surveillance inspections of Time to Market's gains?
<--- Score

32. What are customers monitoring?
<--- Score

33. What are the obstacles to developing and deploying the real-time monitoring tools?
<--- Score

34. What other areas of the group might benefit from the Time to Market team's improvements, knowledge, and learning?
<--- Score

35. Is it necessary to spend time on planning before starting to produce?
<--- Score

36. What is the standard for acceptable Time to Market performance?

<--- Score

37. Is there a transfer of ownership and knowledge to process owner and process team tasked with the responsibilities.
<--- Score

38. Is there a standardized process?
<--- Score

39. Is there a documented and implemented monitoring plan?
<--- Score

40. Is the Time to Market test/monitoring cost justified?
<--- Score

41. Are suggested corrective/restorative actions indicated on the response plan for known causes to problems that might surface?
<--- Score

42. How do you align hiring standards to match external labor market supply to improve quality of hire and decrease time to fill?
<--- Score

43. What should you measure to verify efficiency gains?
<--- Score

44. Is there a control plan in place for sustaining improvements (short and long-term)?
<--- Score

45. What other systems, operations, processes, and infrastructures (hiring practices, staffing, training, incentives/rewards, metrics/dashboards/scorecards, etc.) need updates, additions, changes, or deletions in order to facilitate knowledge transfer and improvements?
<--- Score

46. How might the group capture best practices and lessons learned so as to leverage improvements?
<--- Score

47. What Time to Market standards are applicable?
<--- Score

48. Why do brands, organizations, and professionals alike need to invest time and money in social media listening and monitoring?
<--- Score

49. Will existing staff require re-training, for example, to learn new business processes?
<--- Score

50. How is change control managed?
<--- Score

51. How is Time to Market project cost planned, managed, monitored?
<--- Score

52. Are documented procedures clear and easy to follow for the operators?
<--- Score

53. What quality tools were useful in the control

phase?
<--- Score

54. Does the Time to Market performance meet the customer's requirements?
<--- Score

55. How much time do you plan to devote to trading?
<--- Score

56. What are the gains in terms of productivity, time to market, money, and quality?
<--- Score

57. How will input, process, and output variables be checked to detect for sub-optimal conditions?
<--- Score

58. Do you monitor the effectiveness of your Time to Market activities?
<--- Score

59. Does improved marketing increase market share, which results in increased profits (perhaps from economies of scale), thus providing funds for increased new-product development?
<--- Score

60. Implementation Planning: is a pilot needed to test the changes before a full roll out occurs?
<--- Score

61. Who is the Time to Market process owner?
<--- Score

62. How will the process owner verify improvement in present and future sigma levels, process capabilities?
<--- Score

63. Do the viable solutions scale to future needs?
<--- Score

64. Is a response plan in place for when the input, process, or output measures indicate an 'out-of-control' condition?
<--- Score

65. How will report readings be checked to effectively monitor performance?
<--- Score

66. What is the control/monitoring plan?
<--- Score

67. Is there documentation that will support the successful operation of the improvement?
<--- Score

68. Are new process steps, standards, and documentation ingrained into normal operations?
<--- Score

69. Which social media channels do meeting planners tend to spend the most time on?
<--- Score

70. When is the best time to admit that you violated manufacturer standards?
<--- Score

71. Is knowledge gained on process shared and

institutionalized?
<--- Score

72. Will any special training be provided for results interpretation?
<--- Score

73. Have new or revised work instructions resulted?
<--- Score

74. What is the recommended frequency of auditing?
<--- Score

75. How do you typically plan your day to manage your time effectively?
<--- Score

76. How widespread is its use?
<--- Score

77. Will your goals reflect your program budget?
<--- Score

78. What is the time to market cycle from adoption of standards to installation across the client base?
<--- Score

79. Does the plan provide internal fairness, and how does it measure up to that offered by external competitors seeking to recruit and retain from the same market?
<--- Score

80. Are operating procedures consistent?
<--- Score

Add up total points for this section:
_____ = Total points for this section

Divided by: ______ (number of statements answered) = ______ Average score for this section

Transfer your score to the Time to Market Index at the beginning of the Self-Assessment.

CRITERION #7: SUSTAIN:

INTENT: Retain the benefits.

In my belief, the answer to this question is clearly defined:

5 Strongly Agree

4 Agree

3 Neutral

2 Disagree

1 Strongly Disagree

1. Who is involved with workflow mapping?
<--- Score

2. Where can you break convention?
<--- Score

3. Will the project time to market beat the competition?
<--- Score

4. Why is time to market important?

<--- Score

5. Which functions and people interact with the supplier and or customer?
<--- Score

6. How do you lead with Time to Market in mind?
<--- Score

7. What is your current time to market on your products?
<--- Score

8. How do customers see your organization?
<--- Score

9. Why reduced time to market, reduced cycle time, and first-mover status are considered important B2C e-commerce objectives?
<--- Score

10. What is the best number and time for you to call?
<--- Score

11. Is it time to refresh your efforts, too?
<--- Score

12. Do you have the flexibility or associated time to market to execute on strategy and change management internally?
<--- Score

13. What is the appropriate time to execute email campaigns?
<--- Score

14. When is the best time to conduct negotiations?
<--- Score

15. What is the average time to market?
<--- Score

16. How much time can staff dedicate to social media each day and/or each week?
<--- Score

17. Is now a good time to implement?
<--- Score

18. What is the time frame to complete the market Surveillance?
<--- Score

19. What is the best day and time to send email?
<--- Score

20. How do you reduce time to market?
<--- Score

21. Is it time to shift some – or more – of your marketing to new channels as social media and mobile marketing?
<--- Score

22. How do you increase competitiveness in time to market, time to deliver, flexibility and variety?
<--- Score

23. How would you rate knowledge management in your organization?
<--- Score

24. When is the best time of day to send your email?
<--- Score

25. How will you bring the product or service to the market?
<--- Score

26. What is the purpose of Time to Market in relation to the mission?
<--- Score

27. How does autodesk design review speed time to market?
<--- Score

28. What are internal and external Time to Market relations?
<--- Score

29. What does your business hope to gain from social media over what period of time?
<--- Score

30. How is the machine automation system affected when build times are reduced?
<--- Score

31. Are there new tools or technologies available that can save you time?
<--- Score

32. Do you really have what it takes to think about growth all-the-time?
<--- Score

33. Are you willing and physically able to do the extra work and commit the additional time to run a direct marketing operation?
<--- Score

34. Will it make them smarter, accelerate time to market, increase competitive advantage, or serve as a platform for growth?
<--- Score

35. Can operators reduce time to market by innovating current legacy systems into ones that Agile and able to adapt easily to a constantly changing environment?
<--- Score

36. What is the time frame to penetrate the market for the technology versus its competitors?
<--- Score

37. Ask yourself: how would you do this work if you only had one staff member to do it?
<--- Score

38. Do declining discount rates lead to time inconsistent economic advice?
<--- Score

39. Does management devote sufficient time and resources to the hiring and selection of employees?
<--- Score

40. How do you maintain a short time to market?
<--- Score

41. If there were zero limitations, what would you do differently?
<--- Score

42. How do you move to automated testing and deployments so your time to market for change reduces?
<--- Score

43. What is the recommended percentage of a marketers budget and time to dedicate to testing?
<--- Score

44. How do you capture the value associated with time to market and faster innovation?
<--- Score

45. Has the time come to renovate an investment property?
<--- Score

46. Is there a specific time period you want to cover?
<--- Score

47. When is the best time to send an sms?
<--- Score

48. What better time to shift to your organization mentality than the present?
<--- Score

49. How do you see rapid time to market and value in weeks versus months?
<--- Score

50. Is it time for the board to embrace social media?
<--- Score

51. Do you increase product ROI by decreasing the time to market?
<--- Score

52. What is the average amount of time it takes to prepare a vacant unit for occupancy?
<--- Score

53. How do you accelerate your time to market model?
<--- Score

54. What can individual investors do to use social media, while at the same time protecting themselves?
<--- Score

55. Will supporting bluetooth speed up time to market or slow it down?
<--- Score

56. When is the best time to send an email?
<--- Score

57. Are you doing so to reduce time to market?
<--- Score

58. How do you make it meaningful in connecting Time to Market with what users do day-to-day?
<--- Score

59. How do you know when it is time to commercialize?
<--- Score

60. Are you willing to take the time to call buyers for appointments, meet with them, and take free samples to gain credibility?
<--- Score

61. Do producers have timely access to market information provided by the buyer or an indirect actor?
<--- Score

62. How much time are you willing to put in?
<--- Score

63. Is there a system in place to enable real-time updates and reporting?
<--- Score

64. How much time are you willing to devote to your marketing overall?
<--- Score

65. Do you think Time to Market accomplishes the goals you expect it to accomplish?
<--- Score

66. Are you budgeting time to market?
<--- Score

67. How do you ensure that the most important things are sufficiently tested without delaying time to market?
<--- Score

68. If no one would ever find out about your accomplishments, how would you lead differently?
<--- Score

69. How much time have salespeople spent in the last hundred years going back and forth to find a meeting time?
<--- Score

70. How do you help your business partners accomplish faster time to market?
<--- Score

71. Is there anything you can do ahead of time to make providers more receptive to outreach visits?
<--- Score

72. How do you streamline innovations to make faster time to market?
<--- Score

73. Will ai and automation help your organization accelerate time to market for its new products and services?
<--- Score

74. What is worth More - Cutting Time to Market, or Cutting OpeX?
<--- Score

75. What else do you do to streamline the run time?
<--- Score

76. How do you smoothen the software delivery

supply chain, removing all factors contributing friction, in order to accelerate the time to market?
<--- Score

77. Are you attempting to penetrate a new market with a new product for the first time?
<--- Score

78. Are there time limitations due to store hours?
<--- Score

79. How do you know when its time to ask for the sale?
<--- Score

80. How will you ensure you get what you expected?
<--- Score

81. How does software quality affect time-to-market?
<--- Score

82. Does your organization recreation department utilize a full-time marketing coordinator?
<--- Score

83. What is your organizations desired position relative to the market for base pay, total cash compensation, benefits, and total compensation & benefits?
<--- Score

84. Do you have new ideas to share and time to spend to implement them?
<--- Score

85. Do you make progress fast enough to meet the market window?
<--- Score

86. When is the best time and best day to send emails?
<--- Score

87. Where is the best place or what is the best time to engage with you?
<--- Score

88. When would be a better time for you to call back?
<--- Score

89. Is it to leapfrog the competition in terms of time to market and/or quality?
<--- Score

90. What is the right balance between application quality and time to market?
<--- Score

91. What is your favorite time of the day to check social media?
<--- Score

92. How will time influence responses to attitudes about social media?
<--- Score

93. What is the best time for you to drop by?
<--- Score

94. Have you had time to think about retirement?

<--- Score

95. Which individuals, teams or departments will be involved in Time to Market?
<--- Score

96. Did the average of the samples get closer to the real number each time you added another sample?
<--- Score

97. Why would people want to see pictures of a lot of good looking people having a good time in groups?
<--- Score

98. Are you expecting to generate less-than-full-time jobs?
<--- Score

99. How important is Time to Market to the user organizations mission?
<--- Score

100. Does the program have the budget, time, and resources to use the channel effectively?
<--- Score

101. What Time to Market skills are most important?
<--- Score

102. What specific market share does it have, and what are the realistic market perspectives, timeline, and steps towards reaching a critical mass?
<--- Score

103. How do you know when its time to pass a lead to sales?
<--- Score

104. Is it time to retire the phrase emerging markets?
<--- Score

105. What Time to Market modifications can you make work for you?
<--- Score

106. Do you launch the test (or winning variant) in a reasonable timeframe?
<--- Score

107. How can the enterprise minimize time to market by modifying delivery options on the portfolio?
<--- Score

108. How long will it take to change?
<--- Score

109. What is your delivery lead time/time to market?
<--- Score

110. Who do you want your customers to become?
<--- Score

111. How much time will you be able to dedicate to responding and interacting?
<--- Score

112. What role does communication play in the success or failure of a Time to Market project?
<--- Score

113. What is average time to market for the products/services you are likely to request?
<--- Score

114. What is the reasonable time to keep the summaries of the studies in your organization files?
<--- Score

115. What to achieve over a period of time?
<--- Score

116. How do you know when its time to look for a commercial space?
<--- Score

117. Are there any activities that you can take off your to do list?
<--- Score

118. Were lessons learned captured and communicated?
<--- Score

119. How do you possibly know what time a subscriber is likely to open your emails?
<--- Score

120. How does anyone have enough time to spend on social media?
<--- Score

121. Do the metrics promote new sources of revenues or time to market?
<--- Score

122. What do you do to reduce time to market and deliver more value faster?
<--- Score

123. What is the typical turn-around time for support to get back to clients?
<--- Score

124. What threat is Time to Market addressing?
<--- Score

125. If you recycle content most or all of the time, what motivates you to do this?
<--- Score

126. Does it significantly accelerate the time to market of the business initiative?
<--- Score

127. What is your organizations strategy and goals (e.g., client growth, entering new markets, transition to a regulated organization, adding savings products and services)?
<--- Score

128. What is your prime-time to add photos on Social Media?
<--- Score

129. Is there a time limit to consent?
<--- Score

130. Does your manager have the time to manage and track fees?
<--- Score

131. What are the steps to enhance productivity, efficiency, and time to market of the UAT team with the application of Agile practices?
<--- Score

132. How do you shorten time to market?
<--- Score

133. Is it time to promote your practice?
<--- Score

134. What should be the time-to-market (available for the client)?
<--- Score

135. How is market demand likely to evolve in the coming months?
<--- Score

136. Has it reduced the time to market products?
<--- Score

137. What is your formula for success in Time to Market ?
<--- Score

138. Will there be any necessary staff changes (redundancies or new hires)?
<--- Score

139. Which segments are the most likely to increase in value over time?

<--- Score

140. How much does Time to Market help?
<--- Score

141. How much time to you devote to marketing efforts?
<--- Score

142. Did it help that you have invested so much time in connecting to people through social media?
<--- Score

143. When is the right time to market?
<--- Score

144. Do you have enough freaky customers in your portfolio pushing you to the limit day in and day out?
<--- Score

145. Are you in a position to fulfill your role in times of market distress?
<--- Score

146. Will it increase your software quality and time to market?
<--- Score

147. What have been your experiences in defining long range Time to Market goals?
<--- Score

148. How is implementation research currently incorporated into each of your goals?
<--- Score

149. When is the best time to ask for referrals?
<--- Score

150. What mobile services does your organization use to provide real-time transit information?
<--- Score

151. Are you willing to invest the time to bring customers back to your web site by sending e-mail announcements about new features?
<--- Score

152. What is the economic benefit of rapid time to market?
<--- Score

153. What is the best time of day to take your products?
<--- Score

154. Do you have the time, staff and finances to be involved?
<--- Score

155. Which models, tools and techniques are necessary?
<--- Score

156. When is a good time to ask for a referral online?
<--- Score

157. Where can the crowd be used best to enable your employees to spend more time on highest value activities?

<--- Score

158. What are some time-to-market considerations?
<--- Score

159. How do you predict the stability of your formulations and reduce time to market?
<--- Score

160. How important when you left last time was it to get work again?
<--- Score

161. How do you know when its time to get serious about transitioning?
<--- Score

162. When is the last time you thought about how to evoke emotion in your customers?
<--- Score

163. What is the right amount of time to spend on Social Media?
<--- Score

164. In a project to restructure Time to Market outcomes, which stakeholders would you involve?
<--- Score

165. If you had to rebuild your organization without any traditional competitive advantages (i.e., no killer technology, promising research, innovative product/ service delivery model, etcetera), how would your people have to approach their work and collaborate together in order to create the necessary conditions

for success?
<--- Score

166. How many rooms should be allocated to and protected for each market segment over time?
<--- Score

167. What are the potential basics of Time to Market fraud?
<--- Score

168. How do you set up your social media platforms in a way that will allow the most effective use of your own time?
<--- Score

169. Is time to market weeks to months, or months to years?
<--- Score

170. Do you have the capacity to support new markets people, production capacity, time?
<--- Score

171. What would you do differently next time?
<--- Score

172. How do you keep the product simple enough to ensure short time to market?
<--- Score

173. Do you have the right capabilities and capacities?
<--- Score

174. When is the best time of day to use a light box?

<--- Score

175. Who does what when its time to go?
<--- Score

176. How can technology be better utilized to enable branches to conduct timely marketing of branch programs, collections, and services?
<--- Score

177. If you do not follow, then how to lead?
<--- Score

178. How do you proactively clarify deliverables and Time to Market quality expectations?
<--- Score

179. What better time to discontinue your special charity rates?
<--- Score

180. What tools do you use once you have decided on a Time to Market strategy and more importantly how do you choose?
<--- Score

181. Do you have to complete your studies in a specified time?
<--- Score

182. What is worth taking the time out of your day to go and see?
<--- Score

183. Has in-work benefit reform helped the labour market?

<--- Score

184. How is the click path of a first-time visitor different from that of a returning visitor?
<--- Score

185. How do you get the customer to use more of the product or use it more often?
<--- Score

186. Who are your customers?
<--- Score

187. What could be a better time to increase an investment in your business?
<--- Score

188. Do you see more potential in people than they do in themselves?
<--- Score

189. Are your responses positive or negative?
<--- Score

190. When do you have time to write and market?
<--- Score

191. What are your personal philosophies regarding Time to Market and how do they influence your work?
<--- Score

192. Does it pay to reduce service response times?
<--- Score

193. When is the best time to prepare and send a news release?

<--- Score

194. What is the time to market for a project, product, or product increment?
<--- Score

195. Will the market surveillance portal be accessible to the brand and manufacturer on real time basis?
<--- Score

196. How to avoid pitfalls to shorten the time to market?
<--- Score

197. Who uses your product in ways you never expected?
<--- Score

198. How much time do you have after activity date to complete a claim?
<--- Score

199. Is it easy for customers to withdraw consent at any time?
<--- Score

200. How do you grow the business and speed the time to market with cloud architectures?
<--- Score

201. How much time do you have to spend on your mobile marketing?
<--- Score

202. How do you accelerate your time to market

and time to revenue?
<--- Score

203. Is glue software tested similarly like other product software or does glue software brings some new aspects to integration testing?
<--- Score

204. How much time do you devote to your marketing efforts?
<--- Score

205. Is there a time limit for invoking the statutory option?
<--- Score

206. How do you keep records, of what?
<--- Score

207. What is a good date and time to reschedule the meeting?
<--- Score

208. What makes them interesting and worth your time to open and read?
<--- Score

209. How many mobile apps that take an excessive amount of time to startup have you stopped using?
<--- Score

210. What should you stop doing?
<--- Score

211. Are your products or services always

delivered on time?
<--- Score

212. What strategies are other organizations deploying in order to shorten the time it takes to find talent?
<--- Score

213. Do you care more about productivity or time to market?
<--- Score

214. What is the best time of day (or night) to set up?
<--- Score

215. How do you reduce time to market for future enhancements?
<--- Score

216. How much time do you or others have to devote to keeping the content current?
<--- Score

217. What is the term for a written promise to pay a certain sum of money at a future time?
<--- Score

218. How long time has it taken for your organization to go from idea to market?
<--- Score

219. When is the next time you are available to review your responses?
<--- Score

220. What happens at your organization when people fail?
<--- Score

221. Does your organization value innovation (allows experimentation, encourages questioning of protocol, and maintains open channels of communication)?
<--- Score

222. How can the enterprise minimize time-to-market by modifying delivery options on the portfolio?
<--- Score

223. Do you dedicate specific time to marketing your practice?
<--- Score

224. How related are knowledge management and innovation in your organization and how?
<--- Score

225. When is the right time to order more stock?
<--- Score

226. How does time-to-market compare with industry benchmarks?
<--- Score

227. How do you find the time to consistently post on so many social media platforms?
<--- Score

228. What is the timeline for getting to market?
<--- Score

229. Will there be enough time to establish market traction?
<--- Score

230. How much time does it take before a new style can come on the market and can be manufactured?
<--- Score

231. How often do you deliver on time with quality according to customer expectations?
<--- Score

232. Do you really have time to clean up another mess?
<--- Score

233. Can you do all this work?
<--- Score

234. How do you set Time to Market stretch targets and how do you get people to not only participate in setting these stretch targets but also that they strive to achieve these?
<--- Score

235. How do you ensure that implementations of Time to Market products are done in a way that ensures safety?
<--- Score

236. What are some time management tools and techniques?
<--- Score

237. How is the click path of a first time visitor different to a returning visitor?
<--- Score

238. Who is responsible for ensuring appropriate resources (time, people and money) are allocated to Time to Market?
<--- Score

239. How do you deal with Time to Market changes?
<--- Score

240. Is it possible to maximize return on investment and achieve adequate market share at the same time?
<--- Score

241. When would be a good time to reschedule the meeting?
<--- Score

242. Do Time to Market rules make a reasonable demand on a users capabilities?
<--- Score

243. Do you think you know, or do you know you know ?
<--- Score

244. What knowledge, skills and characteristics mark a good Time to Market project manager?
<--- Score

245. What are the top 3 things at the forefront of your Time to Market agendas for the next 3 years?
<--- Score

246. What is an unauthorized commitment?
<--- Score

247. How well does your organization find the time to keep up with new social media tools and platforms?
<--- Score

248. What is the best time of day to get the most engagement?
<--- Score

249. How do you align delivery of your portfolio, so that your time-to-market is minimized?
<--- Score

250. Is it time to bury the ecosystem concept?
<--- Score

251. What happens if you do not have enough funding?
<--- Score

252. What is your timeframe to meet specific milestones?
<--- Score

253. Are new benefits received and understood?
<--- Score

254. When is the actual time to publish post on social media?
<--- Score

255. Is the impact that Time to Market has shown?

<--- Score

256. How does Time to Market integrate with other stakeholder initiatives?
<--- Score

257. How much time will it take to create and execute the campaign?
<--- Score

258. What would you recommend your friend do if he/ she were facing this dilemma?
<--- Score

259. Do you have time to continue now?
<--- Score

260. Do you get your products to market on time?
<--- Score

261. How does your organization best deliver the right message to the right customer at the right place and time?
<--- Score

262. Think of your Time to Market project, what are the main functions?
<--- Score

263. When is the right time to close your organization?
<--- Score

264. Should income be acknowledged at the time the market value of an asset (liability) increases (decreases), or only when changes in value are

actually converted into cash?
<--- Score

265. What is the time to market trend over time for first delivered product increments?
<--- Score

266. What is a feasible sequencing of reform initiatives over time?
<--- Score

267. How challenging is it to get a real time view of the performance of your estate?
<--- Score

268. Do customer profiles change over time?
<--- Score

269. How would you rate your response time?
<--- Score

270. Is the behavior one-time or continuous?
<--- Score

271. How can any capital market return over any length of time only go up and never down?
<--- Score

272. How can an app encourage shopping time?
<--- Score

273. How do you transition from the baseline to the target?
<--- Score

274. How can time to market be reduced?

<--- Score

275. Who will manage the integration of tools?
<--- Score

276. When is the best time to use a visioning session?
<--- Score

277. Why is it important to know whether value is getting higher or lower over time?
<--- Score

278. Which show is the relationship between the market yields and time to maturity?
<--- Score

279. Are you willing and able to seek and accept full-time work?
<--- Score

280. What is your current time to market and how do you speed it up?
<--- Score

281. What about the capabilities of technologies over time?
<--- Score

282. How many times have you heard people suggesting the best days and times to send your emails?
<--- Score

283. How much time and resources will you invest to manage social media activity?

<--- Score

284. How important is time-to-market?
<--- Score

285. Are you using a design thinking approach and integrating Innovation, Time to Market Experience, and Brand Value?
<--- Score

286. How do you create your products and promote them at the same time?
<--- Score

287. Is time to market the one of the primary product goals?
<--- Score

288. Which segments are closest to your brand and which are more likely to give hard-earned cash or precious time?
<--- Score

289. Who has the time to maintain all that stuff?
<--- Score

290. When information truly is ubiquitous, when reach and connectivity are completely global, when computing resources are infinite, and when a whole new set of impossibilities are not only possible, but happening, what will that do to your business?
<--- Score

291. Is it time to discard the marketing concept?
<--- Score

292. What is the product time to market?
<--- Score

293. Have new benefits been realized?
<--- Score

294. Does skipping test marketing save money?
<--- Score

295. Are you paying enough attention to the partners your company depends on to succeed?
<--- Score

296. What can happen if you have to manage stress for a long time without a break?
<--- Score

297. Are you prepared to devote quality time to assessing potential partners?
<--- Score

298. What are the business goals Time to Market is aiming to achieve?
<--- Score

299. How do you find the time to market your business every day?
<--- Score

300. Is the majority of your time spent on tasks that only you can perform?
<--- Score

301. How much time will be allocated each month to the management of your affiliate program?
<--- Score

302. Do you know who is a friend or a foe?
<--- Score

303. Is there a person that has the time and capability to manage the project internally?
<--- Score

304. How can you become the company that would put you out of business?
<--- Score

305. Do you have some time to move the cartons?
<--- Score

306. Do you know what you are doing? And who do you call if you don't?
<--- Score

307. Will your product make it to the market on time?
<--- Score

308. Are you advertising to a first-time buyer or a loyal customer?
<--- Score

309. Are you seeking to save your team time?
<--- Score

310. Are there activity or time-based triggers in place to convert successfully?
<--- Score

311. How will you motivate the stakeholders with the least vested interest?

<--- Score

312. How much time do you or a member of your team afford to put into social marketing?
<--- Score

313. What are the factors that increase the time to market of new products?
<--- Score

314. What is the time to market trend over time for all final delivered products?
<--- Score

315. What if negotiations for market rent reviews take a long time to agree?
<--- Score

316. When is the best time to promote?
<--- Score

317. What information is critical to your organization that your executives are ignoring?
<--- Score

318. How do you know when the time is right to dive into social media?
<--- Score

319. Is it a good time of day to publish?
<--- Score

320. When is the best time and day of the week to send an email?
<--- Score

321. When is the best time to reach them?
<--- Score

322. What will the anticipated time to market be?
<--- Score

323. Is it time-to-market that is important to you?
<--- Score

324. Are assumptions made in Time to Market stated explicitly?
<--- Score

325. What is the Best Time to Send an Email Promotion or Newsletter?
<--- Score

326. Is now the time to enter the credit markets?
<--- Score

327. What life insurance options are available to part-time and temporary associates?
<--- Score

328. What could be better than having a day off from all your responsibilities and getting some time to relax?
<--- Score

329. What is the average length of time to complete a sale from first contact to receipt of payment?
<--- Score

330. Why not do Time to Market?
<--- Score

331. What better time to ask for a referral than just after you have made them feel important?
<--- Score

332. What is a good day and time for you to meet with your staff?
<--- Score

333. Are you comfortable with the time it may take to grow and sustain your business?
<--- Score

334. What happens if its time to start taking withdrawals during a bear market, when stock and bond prices are declining?
<--- Score

335. Do you feel that more should be done in the Time to Market area?
<--- Score

336. What will your new product marketing strategy be?
<--- Score

337. Do you have the time to be on the phone for a few hours to save yourself a quarter?
<--- Score

338. Will you have staff and time to be consistent?
<--- Score

339. Can devops transform your time to market?
<--- Score

340. When is the best time to email your list?
<--- Score

341. Have benefits been optimized with all key stakeholders?
<--- Score

342. Can reports be posted to portals for all clients simultaneously to save time?
<--- Score

343. What tasks take you a lot of time to complete?
<--- Score

344. How much time do you have to dedicate to running your social media accounts?
<--- Score

345. Do patents have value for an E-Commerce organization or is time to market more important?
<--- Score

346. Do you test only one change at a time?
<--- Score

347. What is your average time to hire?
<--- Score

348. What is the change in time to market?
<--- Score

349. How do you know that mutual funds try to time markets?
<--- Score

350. Will it reduce time to market through reliable

continuous deployment?
<--- Score

351. Have you ever gone without an income for a significant period of time, whilst simultaneously working yourself to the core?
<--- Score

352. How much time do you have after activity date to complete an approved claim?
<--- Score

353. Who is on the team?
<--- Score

354. What do we do when new problems arise?
<--- Score

355. Is early, one-time delivery preferable to a long-term subscription offering?
<--- Score

356. Do people expect to get all of items at the same time?
<--- Score

357. What is the craziest thing you can do?
<--- Score

358. Should legislation also provide for minimum information that should be disclosed to consumers at the time of making a purchase?
<--- Score

359. Which organization could continue to sell product and continue to make a profit for a long

period of time?
<--- Score

360. Is now a good time to proceed with the interview?
<--- Score

361. Are you considered by your employer to be a full-time employee?
<--- Score

362. If you find that you havent accomplished one of the goals for one of the steps of the Time to Market strategy, what will you do to fix it?
<--- Score

363. Is Time to Market dependent on the successful delivery of a current project?
<--- Score

364. Who, on the executive team or the board, has spoken to a customer recently?
<--- Score

365. When was the last time you looked forward to receiving a marketing message?
<--- Score

366. When would be a good time to do that?
<--- Score

367. How do the estimated average life and final maturity compare to your investment time frames?
<--- Score

368. Is there an acceptable balance between time-

to-market pressures and the application of quality principles?
<--- Score

369. How do you shorten time-to-market?
<--- Score

370. Are you willing to give up face time with your customers and trust someone else to sell your products?
<--- Score

371. Does your team spend too much time playing defense?
<--- Score

372. How do you accelerate your time-to-market model?
<--- Score

373. How many times do you give your profits back to the market?
<--- Score

374. What is the desired time to market for new services?
<--- Score

375. Is operating a night-time market different to operating a day-time market?
<--- Score

376. How do you speed time to market?
<--- Score

377. How close are the indices to all-time highs?

<--- Score

378. In the past year, what have you done (or could you have done) to increase the accurate perception of your company/brand as ethical and honest?
<--- Score

379. What might unions stance towards part-time work be?
<--- Score

380. What was the last experiment you ran?
<--- Score

381. What are you willing to invest to keep your computing systems on-line all the time?
<--- Score

382. Can organizations simply follow the market to stay competitive?
<--- Score

383. What do you want your first time visitor to do first?
<--- Score

384. What are the rules and assumptions your industry operates under? What if the opposite were true?
<--- Score

Add up total points for this section:
_____ = Total points for this section

Divided by: ______ (number of statements answered) = ______
Average score for this section

Transfer your score to the Time to Market Index at the beginning of the Self-Assessment.

Time To Market and Managing Projects, Criteria for Project Managers:

1.0 Initiating Process Group: Time To Market

1. Just how important is your work to the overall success of the Time To Market project?

2. Do you understand the communication expectations for this Time To Market project?

3. Do you understand all business (operational), technical, resource and vendor risks associated with the Time To Market project?

4. Will the Time To Market project meet the client requirements, and will it achieve the business success criteria that justified doing the Time To Market project in the first place?

5. Does it make any difference if you am successful?

6. How will you know you did it?

7. During which stage of Risk planning are modeling techniques used to determine overall effects of risks on Time To Market project objectives for high probability, high impact risks?

8. During which stage of Risk planning are risks prioritized based on probability and impact?

9. What will you do?

10. How is each deliverable reviewed, verified, and validated?

11. What were the challenges that you encountered during the execution of a previous Time To Market project that you would not want to repeat?

12. The Time To Market project managers have maximum authority in which type of organization?

13. Which six sigma dmaic phase focuses on why and how defects and errors occur?

14. Have you evaluated the teams performance and asked for feedback?

15. How well did the chosen processes fit the needs of the Time To Market project?

16. What were things that you need to improve?

17. Where must it be done?

18. How will you do it?

19. Professionals want to know what is expected from them what are the deliverables?

20. What do you need to do?

1.1 Project Charter: Time To Market

21. Why is a Time To Market project Charter used?

22. Dependent Time To Market projects: what Time To Market projects must be underway or completed before this Time To Market project can be successful?

23. Where does all this information come from?

24. What are the constraints?

25. Who ise input and support will this Time To Market project require?

26. For whom?

27. Does the Time To Market project need to consider any special capacity or capability issues?

28. Assumptions: what factors, for planning purposes, are you considering to be true?

29. Why use a Time To Market project charter?

30. What is in it for you?

31. What metrics could you look at?

32. What goes into your Time To Market project Charter?

33. Major high-level milestone targets: what events measure progress?

34. Is time of the essence?

35. What material?

36. Customer benefits: what customer requirements does this Time To Market project address?

37. How will you know that a change is an improvement?

38. Pop quiz – which are the same inputs as in the Time To Market project charter?

39. How will you learn more about the process or system you are trying to improve?

40. Are you building in-house ?

1.2 Stakeholder Register: Time To Market

41. How much influence do they have on the Time To Market project?

42. Who are the stakeholders?

43. What opportunities exist to provide communications?

44. Is your organization ready for change?

45. How will reports be created?

46. What & Why?

47. How should employers make voices heard?

48. What are the major Time To Market project milestones requiring communications or providing communications opportunities?

49. What is the power of the stakeholder?

50. Who is managing stakeholder engagement?

51. How big is the gap?

52. Who wants to talk about Security?

1.3 Stakeholder Analysis Matrix: Time To Market

53. Who is most interested in information about the topic and/or has previously initiated interest?

54. Participatory approach: how will key stakeholders participate in the Time To Market project?

55. How to measure the achievement of the Development Objective?

56. Does the stakeholder want to be involved or merely need to be informed about the Time To Market project and its process?

57. What actions can be taken to reduce or mitigate risk?

58. Who will be responsible for managing the outcome?

59. Technology development and innovation?

60. Environmental effects?

61. Who has the power to influence the outcomes of the work?

62. What obstacles does your organization face?

63. Where are the good opportunities facing your organizations development?

64. Guiding question: who shall you involve in the making of the stakeholder map?

65. Partnerships, agencies, distribution?

66. Innovative aspects?

67. Loss of key staff?

68. Who has not been involved up to now and should have been?

69. Information and research?

70. Organizational Applicability?

71. Resource providers; who can provide resources to ensure the implementation of the Time To Market project?

72. Which conditions out of the control of the management are crucial to contribute for the achievement of the development objective?

2.0 Planning Process Group: Time To Market

73. You are creating your WBS and find that you keep decomposing tasks into smaller and smaller units. How can you tell when you are done?

74. How well did the chosen processes fit the needs of the Time To Market project?

75. Does it make any difference if you are successful?

76. If task x starts two days late, what is the effect on the Time To Market project end date?

77. How are the principles of aid effectiveness (ownership, alignment, management for development results and mutual responsibility) being applied in the Time To Market project?

78. Is the pace of implementing the products of the program ensuring the completeness of the results of the Time To Market project?

79. How should needs be met?

80. If you are late, will anybody notice?

81. Is the duration of the program sufficient to ensure a cycle that will Time To Market project the sustainability of the interventions?

82. If a task is partitionable, is this a sufficient

condition to reduce the Time To Market project duration?

83. Are the necessary foundations in place to ensure the sustainability of the results of the Time To Market project?

84. Is the Time To Market project making progress in helping to achieve the set results?

85. To what extent has the intervention strategy been adapted to the areas of intervention in which it is being implemented?

86. To what extent are the participating departments coordinating with each other?

87. If action is called for, what form should it take?

88. How can you tell when you are done?

89. How well defined and documented are the Time To Market project management processes you chose to use?

90. Is the Time To Market project supported by national and/or local organizations?

91. To what extent are the visions and actions of the partners consistent or divergent with regard to the program?

2.1 Project Management Plan: Time To Market

92. What is the justification?

93. What is risk management?

94. Is the budget realistic?

95. What goes into your Time To Market project Charter?

96. What if, for example, the positive direction and vision of your organization causes expected trends to change resulting in greater need than expected?

97. What are the training needs?

98. If the Time To Market project management plan is a comprehensive document that guides you in Time To Market project execution and control, then what should it NOT contain?

99. Are there any scope changes proposed for a previously authorized Time To Market project?

100. Are comparable cost estimates used for comparing, screening and selecting alternative plans, and has a reasonable cost estimate been developed for the recommended plan?

101. Are calculations and results of analyzes essentially correct?

102. Are the proposed Time To Market project purposes different than a previously authorized Time To Market project?

103. Are alternatives safe, functional, constructible, economical, reasonable and sustainable?

104. Are there any Client staffing expectations?

105. How do you manage integration?

106. Is there an incremental analysis/cost effectiveness analysis of proposed mitigation features based on an approved method and using an accepted model?

107. Do there need to be organizational changes?

108. What data/reports/tools/etc. do program managers need?

109. Why Change?

110. When is a Time To Market project management plan created?

2.2 Scope Management Plan: Time To Market

111. Are you meeting with stake holders and team members?

112. Have stakeholder accountabilities & responsibilities been clearly defined?

113. Is an industry recognized mechanized support tool(s) being used for Time To Market project scheduling & tracking?

114. Are vendor invoices audited for accuracy before payment?

115. Has a sponsor been identified?

116. Are Time To Market project team members involved in detailed estimating and scheduling?

117. Is it possible to track all classes of Time To Market project work (e.g. scheduled, un-scheduled, defect repair, etc.)?

118. Are milestone deliverables effectively tracked and compared to Time To Market project plan?

119. Without-plan conditions?

120. Can each item be appropriately scheduled?

121. Are adequate resources provided for the quality

assurance function?

122. Does all Time To Market project documentation reside in a common repository for easy access?

123. How many changes are you making?

124. Are Time To Market project team members committed fulltime?

125. How much money have you spent?

126. Is a pmo (Time To Market project management office) in place and provide oversight to the Time To Market project?

127. Is there a formal set of procedures supporting Stakeholder Management?

128. What threats might prevent you from getting there?

129. Has the Time To Market project scope been baselined?

130. Are Time To Market project contact logs kept up to date?

2.3 Requirements Management Plan: Time To Market

131. How knowledgeable is the team in the proposed application area?

132. How will unresolved questions be handled once approval has been obtained?

133. Who will perform the analysis?

134. Did you use declarative statements?

135. Does the Time To Market project have a Change Control process?

136. How detailed should the Time To Market project get?

137. How will the requirements become prioritized?

138. Who has the authority to reject Time To Market project requirements?

139. Could inaccurate or incomplete requirements in this Time To Market project create a serious risk for the business?

140. Did you avoid subjective, flowery or non-specific statements?

141. Is the user satisfied?

142. Why manage requirements?

143. Who is responsible for monitoring and tracking the Time To Market project requirements?

144. How often will the reporting occur?

145. After the requirements are gathered and set forth on the requirements register, theyre little more than a laundry list of items. Some may be duplicates, some might conflict with others and some will be too broad or too vague to understand. Describe how the requirements will be analyzed. Who will perform the analysis?

146. To see if a requirement statement is sufficiently well-defined, read it from the developers perspective. Mentally add the phrase, call me when youre done to the end of the requirement and see if that makes you nervous. In other words, would you need additional clarification from the author to understand the requirement well enough to design and implement it?

147. How will you develop the schedule of requirements activities?

148. Is stakeholder risk tolerance an important factor for the requirements process in this Time To Market project?

149. What is a problem?

150. Who will initially review the Time To Market project work or products to ensure it meets the applicable acceptance criteria?

2.4 Requirements Documentation: Time To Market

151. What images does it conjure?

152. Verifiability. can the requirements be checked?

153. Have the benefits identified with the system being identified clearly?

154. Who is involved?

155. How much does requirements engineering cost?

156. What marketing channels do you want to use: e-mail, letter or sms?

157. Can the requirements be checked?

158. How much testing do you need to do to prove that your system is safe?

159. Do your constraints stand?

160. Are all functions required by the customer included?

161. Completeness. are all functions required by the customer included?

162. How do you get the user to tell you what they want?

163. Are there legal issues?

164. Is the origin of the requirement clearly stated?

165. How do you know when a Requirement is accurate enough?

166. How to document system requirements?

167. What facilities must be supported by the system?

168. How will requirements be documented and who signs off on them?

169. Who is interacting with the system?

170. What are the potential disadvantages/ advantages?

2.5 Requirements Traceability Matrix: Time To Market

171. Is there a requirements traceability process in place?

172. How small is small enough?

173. Describe the process for approving requirements so they can be added to the traceability matrix and Time To Market project work can be performed. Will the Time To Market project requirements become approved in writing?

174. Why use a WBS?

175. Will you use a Requirements Traceability Matrix?

176. What is the WBS?

177. How do you manage scope?

178. What percentage of Time To Market projects are producing traceability matrices between requirements and other work products?

179. What are the chronologies, contingencies, consequences, criteria?

180. Why do you manage scope?

181. How will it affect the stakeholders personally in career?

182. Do you have a clear understanding of all subcontracts in place?

2.6 Project Scope Statement: Time To Market

183. If you were to write a list of what should not be included in the scope statement, what are the things that you would recommend be described as out-of-scope?

184. Will all Time To Market project issues be unconditionally tracked through the issue resolution process?

185. What is change?

186. Have you been able to easily identify success criteria and create objective measurements for each of the Time To Market project scopes goal statements?

187. Risks?

188. What process would you recommend for creating the Time To Market project scope statement?

189. Why do you need to manage scope?

190. Change management vs. change leadership - what is the difference?

191. Identify how your team and you will create the Time To Market project scope statement and the work breakdown structure (WBS). Document how you will create the Time To Market project scope statement and WBS, and make sure you answer the following

questions: In defining Time To Market project scope and the WBS, will you and your Time To Market project team be using methods defined by your organization, methods defined by the Time To Market project management office (PMO), or other methods?

192. If there is an independent oversight contractor, have they signed off on the Time To Market project Plan?

193. Time To Market project lead, team lead, solution architect?

194. How often will scope changes be reviewed?

195. Elements of scope management that deal with concept development ?

196. Will tasks be marked complete only after QA has been successfully completed?

197. Any new risks introduced or old risks impacted. Are there issues that could affect the existing requirements for the result, service, or product if the scope changes?

198. Do you anticipate new stakeholders joining the Time To Market project over time?

199. Will there be a Change Control Process in place?

200. Is there a baseline plan against which to measure progress?

201. Will all tasks resulting from issues be entered into the Time To Market project Plan and tracked through

the plan?

202. Is the Time To Market project organization documented and on file?

2.7 Assumption and Constraint Log: Time To Market

203. Can the requirements be traced to the appropriate components of the solution, as well as test scripts?

204. Have Time To Market project management standards and procedures been established and documented?

205. What other teams / processes would be impacted by changes to the current process, and how?

206. Should factors be unpredictable over time?

207. How do you design an auditing system?

208. Security analysis has access to information that is sanitized?

209. Have the scope, objectives, costs, benefits and impacts been communicated to all involved and/or impacted stakeholders and work groups?

210. What do you audit?

211. Is there documentation of system capability requirements, data requirements, environment requirements, security requirements, and computer and hardware requirements?

212. Have adequate resources been provided by

management to ensure Time To Market project success?

213. Does the system design reflect the requirements?

214. Are there standards for code development?

215. Model-building: what data-analytic strategies are useful when building proportional-hazards models?

216. Are there nonconformance issues?

217. Are there processes defining how software will be developed including development methods, overall timeline for development, software product standards, and traceability?

218. Was the document/deliverable developed per the appropriate or required standards (for example, Institute of Electrical and Electronics Engineers standards)?

219. No superfluous information or marketing narrative?

220. Does a documented Time To Market project organizational policy & plan (i.e. governance model) exist?

221. Are there ways to reduce the time it takes to get something approved?

222. What do you log?

2.8 Work Breakdown Structure: Time To Market

223. Where does it take place?

224. Is the work breakdown structure (wbs) defined and is the scope of the Time To Market project clear with assigned deliverable owners?

225. Do you need another level?

226. When do you stop?

227. When would you develop a Work Breakdown Structure?

228. How will you and your Time To Market project team define the Time To Market projects scope and work breakdown structure?

229. Who has to do it?

230. How far down?

231. When does it have to be done?

232. What has to be done?

233. What is the probability that the Time To Market project duration will exceed xx weeks?

234. What is the probability of completing the Time To Market project in less that xx days?

235. How much detail?

236. Is it a change in scope?

237. Why is it useful?

238. How big is a work-package?

239. Can you make it?

2.9 WBS Dictionary: Time To Market

240. Does the scheduling system provide for the identification of work progress against technical and other milestones, and also provide for forecasts of completion dates of scheduled work?

241. Budgeted cost for work performed?

242. Contemplated overhead expenditure for each period based on the best information currently available?

243. Are material costs reported within the same period as that in which BCWP is earned for that material?

244. Are the contractors estimates of costs at completion reconcilable with cost data reported to us?

245. Are management actions taken to reduce indirect costs when there are significant adverse variances?

246. Should you have a test for each code module?

247. Are data elements reconcilable between internal summary reports and reports forwarded to us?

248. Are the wbs and organizational levels for application of the Time To Market projected overhead costs identified?

249. Are the responsibilities and authorities of each of the above organizational elements or managers clearly defined?

250. How many levels?

251. Are overhead budgets and costs being handled according to the disclosure statement when applicable, or otherwise properly classified (for example, engineering overhead, IR&D)?

252. Are the latest revised estimates of costs at completion compared with the established budgets at appropriate levels and causes of variances identified?

253. Does the contractors system provide for the determination of cost variances attributable to the excess usage of material?

254. Is budgeted cost for work performed calculated in a manner consistent with the way work is planned?

255. Major functional areas of contract effort?

256. Are procedures established to prevent changes to the contract budget base other than the already stated authorized by contractual action?

257. Does the scheduling system identify in a timely manner the status of work?

258. Are the bases and rates for allocating costs from each indirect pool consistently applied?

259. Intermediate schedules, as required, which

provide a logical sequence from the master schedule to the control account level?

2.10 Schedule Management Plan: Time To Market

260. Have all unresolved risks been documented?

261. Has a structured approach been used to break work effort into manageable components (WBS)?

262. Are tasks tracked by hours?

263. Pareto diagrams, statistical sampling, flow charting or trend analysis used quality monitoring?

264. Will the Time To Market project sponsor be involved in preliminary schedule reviews?

265. Are all activities logically sequenced?

266. Have external dependencies been captured in the schedule?

267. Are corrective actions and variances reported?

268. Does the Time To Market project have quality set of schedule BOEs?

269. Are any non-compliance issues that exist due to your organizations practices communicated to your organization?

270. Are assumptions being identified, recorded, analyzed, qualified and closed?

271. Has a provision been made to reassess Time To Market project risks at various Time To Market project stages?

272. Have the key elements of a coherent Time To Market project management strategy been established?

273. Have activity relationships and interdependencies within tasks been adequately identified?

274. Is the plan consistent with industry best practices?

275. Are the primary and secondary schedule tools defined?

276. Are the appropriate IT resources adequate to meet planned commitments?

277. Is there any form of automated support for Issues Management?

278. Have Time To Market project success criteria been defined?

2.11 Activity List: Time To Market

279. What went wrong?

280. When do the individual activities need to start and finish?

281. How do you determine the late start (LS) for each activity?

282. How should ongoing costs be monitored to try to keep the Time To Market project within budget?

283. What is the probability the Time To Market project can be completed in xx weeks?

284. How will it be performed?

285. For other activities, how much delay can be tolerated?

286. Should you include sub-activities?

287. What did not go as well?

288. The wbs is developed as part of a joint planning session. and how do you know that youhave done this right?

289. What went well?

290. What will be performed?

291. When will the work be performed?

292. How detailed should a Time To Market project get?

293. In what sequence?

294. Where will it be performed?

295. How can the Time To Market project be displayed graphically to better visualize the activities?

296. What is the LF and LS for each activity?

297. Is there anything planned that does not need to be here?

298. Who will perform the work?

2.12 Activity Attributes: Time To Market

299. What is your organizations history in doing similar activities?

300. How many days do you need to complete the work scope with a limit of X number of resources?

301. Do you feel very comfortable with your prediction?

302. What conclusions/generalizations can you draw from this?

303. Have you identified the Activity Leveling Priority code value on each activity?

304. How difficult will it be to do specific activities on this Time To Market project?

305. What is missing?

306. How much activity detail is required?

307. Can you re-assign any activities to another resource to resolve an over-allocation?

308. What went right?

309. Is there a trend during the year?

310. Where else does it apply?

311. How do you manage time?

312. Would you consider either of corresponding activities an outlier?

313. Activity: what is In the Bag?

314. How many resources do you need to complete the work scope within a limit of X number of days?

315. Are the required resources available?

316. Have constraints been applied to the start and finish milestones for the phases?

2.13 Milestone List: Time To Market

317. Describe your organizations strengths and core competencies. What factors will make your organization succeed?

318. New USPs?

319. Marketing - reach, distribution, awareness?

320. How soon can the activity start?

321. What would happen if a delivery of material was one week late?

322. Competitive advantages?

323. Legislative effects?

324. Describe the industry you are in and the market growth opportunities. What is the market for your technology, product or service?

325. What specific improvements did you make to the Time To Market project proposal since the previous time?

326. Describe the concept of the technology, product or service that will be or has been developed. How will it be used?

327. Milestone pages should display the UserID of the person who added the milestone. Does a report or query exist that provides this audit information?

328. Insurmountable weaknesses?

329. Gaps in capabilities?

330. Vital contracts and partners?

331. Who will manage the Time To Market project on a day-to-day basis?

332. How late can the activity start?

333. How will the milestone be verified?

334. Reliability of data, plan predictability?

2.14 Network Diagram: Time To Market

335. Are you on time?

336. What job or jobs precede it?

337. What activities must occur simultaneously with this activity?

338. What can be done concurrently?

339. What are the Key Success Factors?

340. If x is long, what would be the completion time if you break x into two parallel parts of y weeks and z weeks?

341. Will crashing x weeks return more in benefits than it costs?

342. What is the lowest cost to complete this Time To Market project in xx weeks?

343. What is the probability of completing the Time To Market project in less that xx days?

344. Which type of network diagram allows you to depict four types of dependencies?

345. What are the Major Administrative Issues?

346. What job or jobs follow it?

347. What job or jobs could run concurrently?

348. If a current contract exists, can you provide the vendor name, contract start, and contract expiration date?

349. What activity must be completed immediately before this activity can start?

350. Why must you schedule milestones, such as reviews, throughout the Time To Market project?

351. Review the logical flow of the network diagram. Take a look at which activities you have first and then sequence the activities. Do they make sense?

352. What controls the start and finish of a job?

2.15 Activity Resource Requirements: Time To Market

353. Are there unresolved issues that need to be addressed?

354. Anything else?

355. When does monitoring begin?

356. Other support in specific areas?

357. How do you handle petty cash?

358. What is the Work Plan Standard?

359. Time for overtime?

360. What are constraints that you might find during the Human Resource Planning process?

361. Which logical relationship does the PDM use most often?

362. Do you use tools like decomposition and rolling-wave planning to produce the activity list and other outputs?

363. Why do you do that?

364. How many signatures do you require on a check and does this match what is in your policy and procedures?

2.16 Resource Breakdown Structure: Time To Market

365. What is the purpose of assigning and documenting responsibility?

366. Why do you do it?

367. How can this help you with team building?

368. What is the difference between % Complete and % work?

369. When do they need the information?

370. Who will use the system?

371. Any changes from stakeholders?

372. What defines a successful Time To Market project?

373. What is the primary purpose of the human resource plan?

374. Who is allowed to see what data about which resources?

375. Which resources should be in the resource pool?

376. What is each stakeholders desired outcome for the Time To Market project?

377. How should the information be delivered?

378. Who needs what information?

379. What is Time To Market project communication management?

2.17 Activity Duration Estimates: Time To Market

380. Are changes to the scope managed according to defined procedures?

381. Account for the make-or-buy process and how to perform the financial calculations involved in the process. What are the main types of contracts if you do decide to outsource?

382. Is training acquired to enhance the skills, knowledge and capabilities of the Time To Market project team?

383. Why should Time To Market project managers strive to make jobs look easy?

384. How can others help Time To Market project managers understand your organizational context for Time To Market projects?

385. Time To Market project manager is using weighted average duration estimates to perform schedule network analysis. Which type of mathematical analysis is being used?

386. Is corrective action taken to bring Time To Market project performance into line with the Time To Market project plan?

387. Are costs that may be needed to account for Time To Market project risks determined?

388. Does a process exist to identify Time To Market project roles, responsibilities and reporting relationships?

389. Are actual Time To Market project results compared with planned or expected results to determine the variance?

390. Which is the BEST Time To Market project management tool to use to determine the longest time the Time To Market project will take?

391. How can you use Microsoft Time To Market project and Excel to assist in Time To Market project risk management?

392. Which does one need in order to complete schedule development?

393. Do your results resemble a normal distribution?

394. How much time is required to develop it?

395. What does it mean to take a systems view of a Time To Market project?

396. Is a contract change control system defined to manage changes to contract terms and conditions?

397. How does Time To Market project management relate to other disciplines?

398. Are training needs identified when resources do not have the required skills to complete Time To Market project activities?

399. Are procurement documents used to solicit accurate and complete proposals from prospective sellers?

2.18 Duration Estimating Worksheet: Time To Market

400. Do any colleagues have experience with your organization and/or RFPs?

401. Science = process: remember the scientific method?

402. What is cost and Time To Market project cost management?

403. Why estimate time and cost?

404. Can the Time To Market project be constructed as planned?

405. What questions do you have?

406. Is a construction detail attached (to aid in explanation)?

407. Define the work as completely as possible. What work will be included in the Time To Market project?

408. What info is needed?

409. Value pocket identification & quantification what are value pockets?

410. How can the Time To Market project be displayed graphically to better visualize the activities?

411. Why estimate costs?

412. What is the total time required to complete the Time To Market project if no delays occur?

413. Does the Time To Market project provide innovative ways for stakeholders to overcome obstacles or deliver better outcomes?

414. What work will be included in the Time To Market project?

415. What utility impacts are there?

416. What is an Average Time To Market project?

2.19 Project Schedule: Time To Market

417. How can you address that situation?

418. Are procedures defined by which the Time To Market project schedule may be changed?

419. Why do you think schedule issues often cause the most conflicts on Time To Market projects?

420. Understand the constraints used in preparing the schedule. Are activities connected because logic dictates the order in which others occur?

421. Are all remaining durations correct?

422. If there are any qualifying green components to this Time To Market project, what portion of the total Time To Market project cost is green?

423. Are activities connected because logic dictates the order in which others occur?

424. If you can not fix it, how do you do it differently?

425. Did the Time To Market project come in under budget?

426. Are key risk mitigation strategies added to the Time To Market project schedule?

427. How can you fix it?

428. How closely did the initial Time To Market project

Schedule compare with the actual schedule?

429. How do you manage Time To Market project Risk?

430. How detailed should a Time To Market project get?

431. Are the original Time To Market project schedule and budget realistic?

432. Your Time To Market project management plan results in a Time To Market project schedule that is too long. If the Time To Market project network diagram cannot change and you have extra personnel resources, what is the BEST thing to do?

2.20 Cost Management Plan: Time To Market

433. Are decisions captured in a decisions log?

434. Have all team members been part of identifying risks?

435. Have the key elements of a coherent Time To Market project management strategy been established?

436. Are all payments made according to the contract(s)?

437. Is it possible to track all classes of Time To Market project work (e.g. scheduled, un-scheduled, defect repair, etc.)?

438. How do you manage cost?

439. Were Time To Market project team members involved in the development of activity & task decomposition?

440. Is an industry recognized mechanized support tool(s) being used for Time To Market project scheduling & tracking?

441. What would the life cycle costs be?

442. Outside experts?

443. Cost tracking and performance analysis – How will cost tracking and performance analysis be accomplished?

444. Schedule variances – how will schedule variances be identified and corrected?

445. Cost variances – how will cost variances be identified and corrected?

446. Were Time To Market project team members involved in detailed estimating and scheduling?

447. Have lessons learned been conducted after each Time To Market project release?

448. Are non-critical path items updated and agreed upon with the teams?

449. Are all vendor contracts closed out?

2.21 Activity Cost Estimates: Time To Market

450. Measurable - are the targets measurable?

451. Does the estimator have experience?

452. Estimated cost?

453. What is the activity inventory?

454. Certification of actual expenditures?

455. Were escalated issues resolved promptly?

456. Were the tasks or work products prepared by the consultant useful?

457. How do you fund change orders?

458. Will you need to provide essential services information about activities?

459. Who determines when the contractor is paid?

460. How do you treat administrative costs in the activity inventory?

461. What happens if you cannot produce the documentation for the single audit?

462. Did the consultant work with local staff to develop local capacity?

463. Were the costs or charges reasonable?

464. What are you looking for?

465. Which contract type places the most risk on the seller?

466. How quickly can the task be done with the skills available?

467. What do you want to know about the stay to know if costs were inappropriately high or low?

468. Can you delete activities or make them inactive?

2.22 Cost Estimating Worksheet: Time To Market

469. Who is best positioned to know and assist in identifying corresponding factors?

470. Ask: are others positioned to know, are others credible, and will others cooperate?

471. What can be included?

472. What happens to any remaining funds not used?

473. Is it feasible to establish a control group arrangement?

474. What additional Time To Market project(s) could be initiated as a result of this Time To Market project?

475. Can a trend be established from historical performance data on the selected measure and are the criteria for using trend analysis or forecasting methods met?

476. Identify the timeframe necessary to monitor progress and collect data to determine how the selected measure has changed?

477. What is the purpose of estimating?

478. Will the Time To Market project collaborate with the local community and leverage resources?

479. What costs are to be estimated?

480. How will the results be shared and to whom?

481. Does the Time To Market project provide innovative ways for stakeholders to overcome obstacles or deliver better outcomes?

482. What will others want?

483. What is the estimated labor cost today based upon this information?

484. Is the Time To Market project responsive to community need?

2.23 Cost Baseline: Time To Market

485. Time To Market project goals -should others be reconsidered?

486. Review your risk triggers -have your risks changed?

487. What does a good WBS NOT look like?

488. Have all the product or service deliverables been accepted by the customer?

489. Escalation criteria met?

490. Who will use corresponding metrics ?

491. What is the most important thing to do next to make your Time To Market project successful?

492. Pcs for your new business. what would the life cycle costs be?

493. Are procedures defined by which the cost baseline may be changed?

494. How long are you willing to wait before you find out were late?

495. Does a process exist for establishing a cost baseline to measure Time To Market project performance?

496. Does the suggested change request represent a

desired enhancement to the products functionality?

497. Has training and knowledge transfer of the operations organization been completed?

498. Has the documentation relating to operation and maintenance of the product(s) or service(s) been delivered to, and accepted by, operations management?

499. Are there contingencies or conditions related to the acceptance?

500. How fast?

501. Is the requested change request a result of changes in other Time To Market project(s)?

502. Vac -variance at completion, how much over/ under budget do you expect to be?

503. How likely is it to go wrong?

2.24 Quality Management Plan: Time To Market

504. What are your organizations current levels and trends for the already stated measures related to customer satisfaction/ dissatisfaction and product/ service performance?

505. Were there any deficiencies / issues identified in the prior years self-assessment?

506. Are qmps good forever?

507. You know what your customers expectations are regarding this process?

508. How will you know that a change is actually an improvement?

509. What data do you gather/use/compile?

510. How do you check in-coming sample material?

511. Does the program use other agents to collect samples?

512. When reporting to different audiences, do you vary the form or type of report?

513. Does the program conduct field testing?

514. Are there trends or hot spots?

515. Have adequate resources been provided by management to ensure Time To Market project success?

516. How do you document and correct nonconformances?

517. How many Time To Market project staff does this specific process affect?

518. Would impacts defined serve as impediments?

519. How is staff trained on the recording of field notes?

520. How does your organization ensure the quality, reliability, and user-friendliness of its hardware and software?

521. Contradictory information between document sections?

522. How are your organizations compensation and recognition approaches and the performance management system used to reinforce high performance?

523. How does your organization perform analyzes to assess overall organizational performance and set priorities?

2.25 Quality Metrics: Time To Market

524. What are your organizations next steps?

525. Can visual measures help you to filter visualizations of interest?

526. What metrics do you measure?

527. Should a modifier be included?

528. How should customers provide input?

529. What method of measurement do you use?

530. Is the reporting frequency appropriate?

531. Have alternatives been defined in the event that failure occurs?

532. How do you calculate corresponding metrics?

533. Who notifies stakeholders of normal and abnormal results?

534. Where did complaints, returns and warranty claims come from?

535. What does this tell us?

536. Are quality metrics defined?

537. How can the effectiveness of each of the activities be measured?

538. What about still open problems?

539. What happens if you get an abnormal result?

540. Who is willing to lead?

541. Is there a set of procedures to capture, analyze and act on quality metrics?

542. Were number of defects identified?

543. Has trace of defects been initiated?

2.26 Process Improvement Plan: Time To Market

544. Are there forms and procedures to collect and record the data?

545. What personnel are the champions for the initiative?

546. What is quality and how will you ensure it?

547. What lessons have you learned so far?

548. Everyone agrees on what process improvement is, right?

549. What personnel are the change agents for your initiative?

550. Where do you focus?

551. Are you following the quality standards?

552. Where are you now?

553. What is the return on investment?

554. How do you manage quality?

555. Has a process guide to collect the data been developed?

556. Who should prepare the process improvement

action plan?

557. What is the test-cycle concept?

558. Has the time line required to move measurement results from the points of collection to databases or users been established?

559. Does your process ensure quality?

560. Are you making progress on the goals?

561. Have the frequency of collection and the points in the process where measurements will be made been determined?

2.27 Responsibility Assignment Matrix: Time To Market

562. How cost benefit analysis?

563. Too many is: do all the identified roles need to be routinely informed or only in exceptional circumstances?

564. What are some important Time To Market project communications management tools?

565. Are all authorized tasks assigned to identified organizational elements?

566. Who is the Time To Market project Manager?

567. What are the assumptions?

568. Is work progressively subdivided into detailed work packages as requirements are defined?

569. The anticipated business volume?

570. Is all contract work included in the CWBS?

571. What materials and procurements needed?

572. Are estimates of costs at completion generated in a rational, consistent manner?

573. Are people afraid to let you know when others are under allocated?

574. Is accountability placed at the lowest-possible level within the Time To Market project so that decisions can be made at that level?

575. What does wbs accomplish?

576. Time-phased control account budgets?

577. Budgets assigned to control accounts?

578. Are too many reports done in writing instead of verbally?

579. How many people do you need?

2.28 Roles and Responsibilities: Time To Market

580. Was the expectation clearly communicated?

581. Influence: what areas of organizational decision making are you able to influence when you do not have authority to make the final decision?

582. Who: who is involved?

583. Where are you most strong as a supervisor?

584. Do the values and practices inherent in the culture of your organization foster or hinder the process?

585. Are Time To Market project team roles and responsibilities identified and documented?

586. Are your policies supportive of a culture of quality data?

587. What are your major roles and responsibilities in the area of performance measurement and assessment?

588. What is working well?

589. Does the team have access to and ability to use data analysis tools?

590. Attainable / achievable: the goal is attainable;

can you actually accomplish the goal?

591. Be specific; avoid generalities. Thank you and great work alone are insufficient. What exactly do you appreciate and why?

592. What should you highlight for improvement?

593. What specific behaviors did you observe?

594. To decide whether to use a quality measurement, ask how will you know when it is achieved?

595. How is your work-life balance?

596. What should you do now to ensure that you are meeting all expectations of your current position?

597. Do you take the time to clearly define roles and responsibilities on Time To Market project tasks?

598. Key conclusions and recommendations: Are conclusions and recommendations relevant and acceptable?

2.29 Human Resource Management Plan: Time To Market

599. Are the people assigned to the Time To Market project sufficiently qualified?

600. Is the steering committee active in Time To Market project oversight?

601. Are multiple estimation methods being employed?

602. Have key stakeholders been identified?

603. Is there a Quality Management Plan?

604. Are governance roles and responsibilities documented?

605. Are all key components of a Quality Assurance Plan present?

606. Are procurement deliverables arriving on time and to specification?

607. How will the Time To Market project manage expectations & meet needs and requirements?

608. Is the Time To Market project sponsor clearly communicating the business case or rationale for why this Time To Market project is needed?

609. How can below standard performers be guided/

developed to upgrade performance?

610. Have lessons learned been conducted after each Time To Market project release?

611. Specific - is the objective clear in terms of what, how, when, and where the situation will be changed?

612. How are you going to ensure that you have a well motivated workforce?

613. How complete is the human resource management plan?

614. Is Time To Market project status reviewed with the steering and executive teams at appropriate intervals?

615. Does the business case include how the Time To Market project aligns with your organizations strategic goals & objectives?

616. Account for the purpose of this Time To Market project by describing, at a high-level, what will be done. What is this Time To Market project aiming to achieve?

2.30 Communications Management Plan: Time To Market

617. Why do you manage communications?

618. In your work, how much time is spent on stakeholder identification?

619. What communications method?

620. Are the stakeholders getting the information others need, are others consulted, are concerns addressed?

621. How do you manage communications?

622. Why is stakeholder engagement important?

623. Are there common objectives between the team and the stakeholder?

624. How is this initiative related to other portfolios, programs, or Time To Market projects?

625. How were corresponding initiatives successful?

626. Who to learn from?

627. Are others part of the communications management plan?

628. Who are the members of the governing body?

629. Who to share with?

630. What help do you and your team need from the stakeholder?

631. Conflict resolution -which method when?

632. Do you ask; can you recommend others for you to talk with about this initiative?

633. Who needs to know and how much?

634. What to learn?

635. Can you think of other people who might have concerns or interests?

636. What steps can you take for a positive relationship?

2.31 Risk Management Plan: Time To Market

637. People risk -are people with appropriate skills available to help complete the Time To Market project?

638. Which risks should get the attention?

639. Are certain activities taking a long time to complete?

640. Do you manage the process through use of metrics?

641. What other risks are created by choosing an avoidance strategy?

642. How would you suggest monitoring for risk transition indicators?

643. Are flexibility and reuse paramount?

644. Have customers been involved fully in the definition of requirements?

645. Is there anything you would now do differently on your Time To Market project based on this experience?

646. Can the risk be avoided by choosing a different alternative?

647. Are there risks to human health or the environment that need to be controlled or mitigated?

648. Is a software Time To Market project management tool available?

649. How do you manage Time To Market project Risk?

650. Can it be changed quickly?

651. User involvement: do you have the right users?

652. Are some people working on multiple Time To Market projects?

653. Are you on schedule?

654. What would you do?

655. Is the number of people on the Time To Market project team adequate to do the job?

656. Why do you want risk management?

2.32 Risk Register: Time To Market

657. Preventative actions - planned actions to reduce the likelihood a risk will occur and/or reduce the seriousness should it occur. What should you do now?

658. Are there any gaps in the evidence?

659. How could corresponding Risk affect the Time To Market project in terms of cost and schedule?

660. When is it going to be done?

661. Are there any knock-on effects/impact on any of the other areas?

662. Contingency actions - planned actions to reduce the immediate seriousness of the risk when it does occur. What should you do when?

663. What risks might negatively or positively affect achieving the Time To Market project objectives?

664. Amongst the action plans and recommendations that you have to introduce are there some that could stop or delay the overall program?

665. How are risks identified?

666. What may happen or not go according to plan?

667. Are implemented controls working as others should?

668. How often will the Risk Management Plan and Risk Register be formally reviewed, and by whom?

669. Methodology: how will risk management be performed on this Time To Market project?

670. Which key risks have ineffective responses or outstanding improvement actions?

671. Is further information required before making a decision?

672. What are the major risks facing the Time To Market project?

673. What evidence do you have to justify the likelihood score of the risk (audit, incident report, claim, complaints, inspection, internal review)?

674. What should you do now?

675. What are your key risks/show istoppers and what is being done to manage them?

676. Budget and schedule: what are the estimated costs and schedules for performing risk-related activities?

2.33 Probability and Impact Assessment: Time To Market

677. Which of corresponding risk factors can be avoided altogether?

678. What is the experience (performance, attitude, business ethics, etc.) in the past with contractors?

679. Mitigation -how can you avoid the risk?

680. Why has this particular mode of contracting been chosen?

681. How will economic events and trends likely affect the Time To Market project?

682. What is the probability of the risk occurring?

683. Are the software tools integrated with each other?

684. Have decisions that should be left open because of inadequate information on technology been identified and responsibility assigned for reducing the uncertainty?

685. Is the customer technically sophisticated in the product area?

686. Which functions, departments, and activities of your organization are going to be affected?

687. Is the customer willing to establish rapid communication links with the developer?

688. Do the requirements require the creation of new algorithms?

689. Anticipated volatility of the requirements?

690. Are staff committed for the duration of the Time To Market project?

691. What risks does the employee encounter?

692. Have you worked with the customer in the past?

693. Are there any Time To Market projects similar to this one in existence?

694. Is the number of people on the Time To Market project team adequate to do the job?

2.34 Probability and Impact Matrix: Time To Market

695. What are the chances the event will occur?

696. Are the best people available?

697. What is your anticipated volatility of the requirements?

698. Prioritized components/features?

699. Will there be an increase in the political conservatism?

700. What are the risks involved in appointing external agencies to manage the Time To Market project?

701. What can you use the analyzed risks for?

702. Workarounds are determined during which risk management process?

703. Are some people working on multiple Time To Market projects?

704. Risk may be made during which step of risk management?

705. Is Time To Market project scope stable?

706. Number of users of the product?

707. Can you handle the investment risk?

708. Amount of reused software?

709. What should be the level of coordination?

710. Are there new risks that mitigation strategies might introduce?

711. Is the present organizational structure for handling the Time To Market project sufficient?

2.35 Risk Data Sheet: Time To Market

712. What do people affected think about the need for, and practicality of preventive measures?

713. Type of risk identified?

714. What is the chance that it will happen?

715. What will be the consequences if the risk happens?

716. What do you know?

717. What can you do?

718. What can happen?

719. What was measured?

720. What is the environment within which you operate (social trends, economic, community values, broad based participation, national directions etc.)?

721. How reliable is the data source?

722. What are the main opportunities available to you that you should grab while you can?

723. What is the likelihood of it happening?

724. Has a sensitivity analysis been carried out?

725. What are you trying to achieve (Objectives)?

726. What were the Causes that contributed?

727. If it happens, what are the consequences?

728. Whom do you serve (customers)?

729. What will be the consequences if it happens?

730. What are you here for (Mission)?

731. Risk of what?

2.36 Procurement Management Plan: Time To Market

732. Are updated Time To Market project time & resource estimates reasonable based on the current Time To Market project stage?

733. Is the steering committee active in Time To Market project oversight?

734. What are your quality assurance overheads?

735. Are the schedule estimates reasonable given the Time To Market project?

736. Are Time To Market project team members involved in detailed estimating and scheduling?

737. Has a quality assurance plan been developed for the Time To Market project?

738. Have the key functions and capabilities been defined and assigned to each release or iteration?

739. Were sponsors and decision makers available when needed outside regularly scheduled meetings?

740. If standardized procurement documents are needed, where can others be found?

741. Does the schedule include Time To Market project management time and change request analysis time?

742. Have all documents been archived in a Time To Market project repository for each release?

743. Do Time To Market project teams & team members report on status / activities / progress?

744. Were Time To Market project team members involved in the development of activity & task decomposition?

745. Are the people assigned to the Time To Market project sufficiently qualified?

746. Are the payment terms being followed?

747. Has the schedule been baselined?

748. Is it possible to track all classes of Time To Market project work (e.g. scheduled, un-scheduled, defect repair, etc.)?

749. Are the Time To Market project plans updated on a frequent basis?

2.37 Source Selection Criteria: Time To Market

750. How can the methods of publicizing the buy be tailored to yield more effective price competition?

751. Who is entitled to a debriefing?

752. Can you make a cost/technical tradeoff?

753. Who must be notified?

754. How do you ensure an integrated assessment of proposals?

755. Is the offeror pricing what is technically proposed?

756. What is the last item a Time To Market project manager must do to finalize Time To Market project close-out?

757. Why promote competition?

758. Comparison of each offers prices to the estimated prices -are there significant differences?

759. How should the preproposal conference be conducted?

760. How is past performance evaluated?

761. When is it appropriate to issue a DRFP?

762. Is there collaboration among your evaluators?

763. What are the limitations on pre-competitive range communications?

764. When and what information can be considered with offerors regarding past performance?

765. When is it appropriate to issue a Draft Request for Proposal (DRFP)?

766. What aspects should the contracting officer brief the Time To Market project on prior to evaluation of proposals?

767. What should be the contracting officers strategy?

768. What does a sample rating scale look like?

769. How will you evaluate offerors proposals?

2.38 Stakeholder Management Plan: Time To Market

770. If a problem has been detected, what tools can be used to determine a root cause?

771. Does the Time To Market project have a formal Time To Market project Plan?

772. What information should be collected?

773. Do you know what your customers expectations are regarding this process?

774. What is the general purpose in defining responsibilities of the already stated affiliated with the Time To Market project?

775. Are internal Time To Market project status meetings held at reasonable intervals?

776. How are the overall Time To Market project development processes to be undertaken to produce the Time To Market project outputs?

777. Is an industry recognized mechanized support tool(s) being used for Time To Market project scheduling & tracking?

778. When would you develop a Time To Market project Execution Plan?

779. What is the primary function of the Activity

Decomposition Decision Tree?

780. Who is responsible for gathering and reporting data for employment?

781. Has the Time To Market project manager been identified?

782. How will the equipment be verified?

783. When would you develop a Time To Market project Business Plan?

784. Are written status reports provided on a designated frequent basis?

785. Is the communication plan being followed?

2.39 Change Management Plan: Time To Market

786. What is the most cynical response it can receive?

787. Different application of an existing process?

788. Readiness -what is a successful end state?

789. What are the essentials of the message?

790. What are the key change management success metrics?

791. Will the culture embrace or reject this change?

792. Will you need new processes?

793. What new behaviours are required?

794. What can you do to minimise misinterpretation and negative perceptions?

795. What are you trying to achieve as a result of communication?

796. How might they respond to the message and if the response may be negative or open to misinterpretation, what else needs to be said?

797. What policies and procedures need to be changed?

798. What type of materials/channels will be available to leverage?

799. Who might be able to help you the most?

800. How badly can information be misinterpreted?

801. How far reaching in your organization is the change?

802. Will the readiness criteria be met prior to the training roll out?

803. How does the principle of senders and receivers make the Time To Market project communications effort more complex?

804. Who should be involved in developing a change management strategy?

3.0 Executing Process Group: Time To Market

805. What is the difference between using brainstorming and the Delphi technique for risk identification?

806. When do you share the scorecard with managers?

807. What is the critical path for this Time To Market project and how long is it?

808. Could a new application negatively affect the current IT infrastructure?

809. How do you measure difficulty?

810. How well did the team follow the chosen processes?

811. Why is it important to determine activity sequencing on Time To Market projects?

812. How does a Time To Market project life cycle differ from a product life cycle?

813. Who will provide training?

814. Will new hardware or software be required for servers or client machines?

815. What are the main types of goods and services

being outsourced?

816. What areas does the group agree are the biggest success on the Time To Market project?

817. Is the program supported by national and/or local organizations?

818. What areas were overlooked on this Time To Market project?

819. How do you prevent staff are just doing busywork to pass the time?

820. Does the Time To Market project team have enough people to execute the Time To Market project plan?

821. How do you control progress of your Time To Market project?

822. What is the difference between conceptual, application, and evaluative questions?

3.1 Team Member Status Report: Time To Market

823. What specific interest groups do you have in place?

824. How will resource planning be done?

825. How does this product, good, or service meet the needs of the Time To Market project and your organization as a whole?

826. Are the products of your organizations Time To Market projects meeting customers objectives?

827. How it is to be done?

828. Why is it to be done?

829. When a teams productivity and success depend on collaboration and the efficient flow of information, what generally fails them?

830. Does every department have to have a Time To Market project Manager on staff?

831. What is to be done?

832. Do you have an Enterprise Time To Market project Management Office (EPMO)?

833. Will the staff do training or is that done by a third party?

834. The problem with Reward & Recognition Programs is that the truly deserving people all too often get left out. How can you make it practical?

835. Are your organizations Time To Market projects more successful over time?

836. Does the product, good, or service already exist within your organization?

837. Does your organization have the means (staff, money, contract, etc.) to produce or to acquire the product, good, or service?

838. How much risk is involved?

839. How can you make it practical?

840. Is there evidence that staff is taking a more professional approach toward management of your organizations Time To Market projects?

841. Are the attitudes of staff regarding Time To Market project work improving?

3.2 Change Request: Time To Market

842. How can you ensure that changes have been made properly?

843. Who can suggest changes?

844. For which areas does this operating procedure apply?

845. Will all change requests and current status be logged?

846. Screen shots or attachments included in a Change Request?

847. Should staff call into the helpdesk or go to the website?

848. Why do you want to have a change control system?

849. What is a Change Request Form?

850. Has the change been highlighted and documented in the CSCI?

851. How shall the implementation of changes be recorded?

852. Who is included in the change control team?

853. Should a more thorough impact analysis be conducted?

854. What type of changes does change control take into account?

855. Are you implementing itil processes?

856. What are the basic mechanics of the Change Advisory Board (CAB)?

857. What is the relationship between requirements attributes and reliability?

858. What are the duties of the change control team?

859. How are changes requested (forms, method of communication)?

860. Has a formal technical review been conducted to assess technical correctness?

861. Why control change across the life cycle?

3.3 Change Log: Time To Market

862. Who initiated the change request?

863. Does the suggested change request seem to represent a necessary enhancement to the product?

864. Will the Time To Market project fail if the change request is not executed?

865. Is the change request within Time To Market project scope?

866. When was the request approved?

867. How does this relate to the standards developed for specific business processes?

868. How does this change affect scope?

869. When was the request submitted?

870. Is the change request open, closed or pending?

871. Is this a mandatory replacement?

872. Where do changes come from?

873. Do the described changes impact on the integrity or security of the system?

874. Is the change backward compatible without limitations?

875. Is the requested change request a result of changes in other Time To Market project(s)?

876. How does this change affect the timeline of the schedule?

877. Is the submitted change a new change or a modification of a previously approved change?

3.4 Decision Log: Time To Market

878. How do you know when you are achieving it?

879. Meeting purpose; why does this team meet?

880. It becomes critical to track and periodically revisit both operational effectiveness; Are you noticing all that you need to, and are you interpreting what you see effectively?

881. At what point in time does loss become unacceptable?

882. How consolidated and comprehensive a story can you tell by capturing currently available incident data in a central location and through a log of key decisions during an incident?

883. Behaviors; what are guidelines that the team has identified that will assist them with getting the most out of team meetings?

884. What are the cost implications?

885. Adversarial environment. is your opponent open to a non-traditional workflow, or will it likely challenge anything you do?

886. Linked to original objective?

887. Who will be given a copy of this document and where will it be kept?

888. How does an increasing emphasis on cost containment influence the strategies and tactics used?

889. How does the use a Decision Support System influence the strategies/tactics or costs?

890. How does provision of information, both in terms of content and presentation, influence acceptance of alternative strategies?

891. Which variables make a critical difference?

892. What alternatives/risks were considered?

893. How do you define success?

894. What was the rationale for the decision?

895. What is the average size of your matters in an applicable measurement?

896. Decision-making process; how will the team make decisions?

897. Who is the decisionmaker?

3.5 Quality Audit: Time To Market

898. Does the suppliers quality system have a written procedure for corrective action when a defect occurs?

899. How does your organization know that its research funding systems are appropriately effective and constructive in enabling quality research outcomes?

900. How does your organization know that its security arrangements are appropriately effective and constructive?

901. How does your organization know that its relationships with relevant professional bodies are appropriately effective and constructive?

902. Why are you trying to do it?

903. Are the review comments incorporated?

904. Are measuring and test equipment that have been placed out of service suitably identified and excluded from use in any device reconditioning operation?

905. How does your organization know that its staff financial services are appropriately effective and constructive?

906. How do you indicate the extent to which your personnel would be expected to contribute to the work effort?

907. How does your organization know that its relationships with other relevant organizations are appropriately effective and constructive?

908. Are all employees including salespersons made aware that they must report all complaints received from any source for inclusion in the complaint handling system?

909. How does your organization know that its promotions system is appropriately effective, constructive and fair?

910. How does your organization know that its management of its ethical responsibilities is appropriately effective and constructive?

911. How does your organization know that its staff embody the core knowledge, skills and characteristics for which it wishes to be recognized?

912. How does your organization know that its advisory services are appropriately effective and constructive?

913. Do the acceptance procedures and specifications include the criteria for acceptance/rejection, define the process to be used, and specify the measuring and test equipment that is to be used?

914. Is the reports overall tone appropriate?

915. How does your organization know that its system for recruiting the best staff possible are appropriately effective and constructive?

916. How does your organization know that its policy management system is appropriately effective and constructive?

917. Have the risks associated with the intentions been identified, analyzed and appropriate responses developed?

3.6 Team Directory: Time To Market

918. Process decisions: is work progressing on schedule and per contract requirements?

919. Who are your stakeholders (customers, sponsors, end users, team members)?

920. Does a Time To Market project team directory list all resources assigned to the Time To Market project?

921. Who should receive information (all stakeholders)?

922. Who will talk to the customer?

923. Who are the Team Members?

924. Process decisions: are contractors adequately prosecuting the work?

925. Process decisions: how well was task order work performed?

926. Process decisions: do job conditions warrant additional actions to collect job information and document on-site activity?

927. Who is the Sponsor?

928. What needs to be communicated?

929. Where will the product be used and/or delivered or built when appropriate?

930. Process decisions: are there any statutory or regulatory issues relevant to the timely execution of work?

931. Timing: when do the effects of communication take place?

932. When will you produce deliverables?

933. How will you accomplish and manage the objectives?

934. Who will be the stakeholders on your next Time To Market project?

935. Have you decided when to celebrate the Time To Market projects completion date?

936. Decisions: what could be done better to improve the quality of the constructed product?

937. What are you going to deliver or accomplish?

3.7 Team Operating Agreement: Time To Market

938. Do you vary your voice pace, tone and pitch to engage participants and gain involvement?

939. Are there more than two national cultures represented by your team?

940. How will you resolve conflict efficiently and respectfully?

941. To whom do you deliver your services?

942. How will group handle unplanned absences?

943. Reimbursements: how will the team members be reimbursed for expenses and time commitments?

944. Are there more than two native languages represented by your team?

945. Do team members need to frequently communicate as a full group to make timely decisions?

946. Do you call or email participants to ensure understanding, follow-through and commitment to the meeting outcomes?

947. Has the appropriate access to relevant data and analysis capability been granted?

948. Communication protocols: how will the team communicate?

949. Are there more than two functional areas represented by your team?

950. Did you delegate tasks such as taking meeting minutes, presenting a topic and soliciting input?

951. Did you draft the meeting agenda?

952. Do you begin with a question to engage everyone?

953. Does your team need access to all documents and information at all times?

954. Are there the right people on your team?

955. How do you want to be thought of and known within your organization?

956. Resource allocation: how will individual team members account for time and expenses, and how will this be allocated in the team budget?

3.8 Team Performance Assessment: Time To Market

957. To what degree will new and supplemental skills be introduced as the need is recognized?

958. When a reviewer complains about method variance, what is the essence of the complaint?

959. To what degree are the members clear on what they are individually responsible for and what they are jointly responsible for?

960. To what degree are fresh input and perspectives systematically caught and added (for example, through information and analysis, new members, and senior sponsors)?

961. To what degree can team members meet frequently enough to accomplish the teams ends?

962. To what degree can the team measure progress against specific goals?

963. When does the medium matter?

964. Can team performance be reliably measured in simulator and live exercises using the same assessment tool?

965. To what degree will team members, individually and collectively, commit time to help themselves and others learn and develop skills?

966. To what degree can team members vigorously define the teams purpose in considerations with others who are not part of the functioning team?

967. To what degree are staff involved as partners in the improvement process?

968. Lack of method variance in self-reported affect and perceptions at work: Reality or artifact?

969. To what degree does the teams approach to its work allow for modification and improvement over time?

970. What makes opportunities more or less obvious?

971. To what degree does the teams work approach provide opportunity for members to engage in fact-based problem solving?

972. Is there a particular method of data analysis that you would recommend as a means of demonstrating that method variance is not of great concern for a given dataset?

973. To what degree will the team ensure that all members equitably share the work essential to the success of the team?

974. Individual task proficiency and team process behavior: what is important for team functioning?

975. To what degree do members understand and articulate the same purpose without relying on ambiguous abstractions?

976. How does Time To Market project termination impact Time To Market project team members?

3.9 Team Member Performance Assessment: Time To Market

977. What is the target group for instruction (e.g., individual and collective or small team instruction)?

978. Who receives a benchmark visit?

979. Verify business objectives. Are they appropriate, and well-articulated?

980. To what extent did the evaluation influence the instructional path, such as with adaptive testing?

981. To what degree do team members frequently explore the teams purpose and its implications?

982. How should adaptive assessments be implemented?

983. What innovations (if any) are developed to realize goals?

984. What is the large, desired outcome?

985. What are the evaluation strategies (e.g., reaction, learning, behavior, results) used. What evaluation results did you have?

986. Are there any safeguards to prevent intentional or unintentional rating errors?

987. What evaluation results do you have?

988. What were the challenges that resulted for training and assessment?

989. What are acceptable governance changes?

990. What kinds of performance factors / elements do you use?

991. How accurately is your plan implemented?

992. To what degree is there a sense that only the team can succeed?

993. Why were corresponding selected?

994. What entity leads the process, selects a potential restructuring option and develops the plan?

3.10 Issue Log: Time To Market

995. Who is the stakeholder?

996. Do you have members of your team responsible for certain stakeholders?

997. How do you manage human resources?

998. What effort will a change need?

999. Which stakeholders can influence others?

1000. What is the impact on the risks?

1001. Who is involved as you identify stakeholders?

1002. Is there an important stakeholder who is actively opposed and will not receive messages?

1003. Who have you worked with in past, similar initiatives?

1004. Are the Time To Market project issues uniquely identified, including to which product they refer?

1005. Are there potential barriers between the team and the stakeholder?

1006. Are you constantly rushing from meeting to meeting?

1007. Persistence; will users learn a work around or will they be bothered every time?

1008. Why do you manage human resources?

1009. Do you often overlook a key stakeholder or stakeholder group?

1010. What does the stakeholder need from the team?

1011. Do you feel more overwhelmed by stakeholders?

1012. Are stakeholder roles recognized by your organization?

1013. How is this initiative related to other portfolios, programs, or Time To Market projects?

1014. What is the impact on the Business Case?

4.0 Monitoring and Controlling Process Group: Time To Market

1015. What are the deliverables?

1016. What business situation is being addressed?

1017. How well did the chosen processes produce the expected results?

1018. Did the Time To Market project team have enough people to execute the Time To Market project plan?

1019. How can you monitor progress?

1020. How to ensure validity, quality and consistency?

1021. Key stakeholders to work with. How many potential communications channels exist on the Time To Market project?

1022. Did the Time To Market project team have the right skills?

1023. Is the program making progress in helping to achieve the set results?

1024. Where is the Risk in the Time To Market project?

1025. What were things that you did very well and want to do the same again on the next Time To Market project?

1026. Is there sufficient time allotted between the general system design and the detailed system design phases?

1027. Accuracy: what design will lead to accurate information?

1028. How is agile Time To Market project management done?

1029. What are the goals of the program?

1030. How is agile program management done?

1031. Is there sufficient funding available for this?

1032. What resources (both financial and non-financial) are available/needed?

1033. How many more potential communications channels were introduced by the discovery of the new stakeholders?

4.1 Project Performance Report: Time To Market

1034. To what degree can the cognitive capacity of individuals accommodate the flow of information?

1035. How can Time To Market project sustainability be maintained?

1036. To what degree does the formal organization make use of individual resources and meet individual needs?

1037. To what degree do team members agree with the goals, relative importance, and the ways in which achievement will be measured?

1038. To what degree does the information network provide individuals with the information they require?

1039. To what degree are the skill areas critical to team performance present?

1040. To what degree do the structures of the formal organization motivate taskrelevant behavior and facilitate task completion?

1041. To what degree are the demands of the task compatible with and converge with the mission and functions of the formal organization?

1042. To what degree is the information network consistent with the structure of the formal organization?

1043. What is the degree to which rules govern information exchange between individuals within your organization?

1044. To what degree do team members articulate the teams work approach?

1045. To what degree are the goals ambitious?

1046. To what degree are sub-teams possible or necessary?

1047. To what degree can the team ensure that all members are individually and jointly accountable for the teams purpose, goals, approach, and work-products?

1048. To what degree are the demands of the task compatible with and converge with the relationships of the informal organization?

1049. To what degree does the teams purpose contain themes that are particularly meaningful and memorable?

4.2 Variance Analysis: Time To Market

1050. Are overhead costs budgets established on a basis consistent with the anticipated direct business base?

1051. Does the contractors system provide unit or lot costs when applicable?

1052. What is the budgeted cost for work scheduled?

1053. What types of services and expense are shared between business segments?

1054. What is the incurrence of actual indirect costs in excess of budgets, by element of expense?

1055. Budget versus actual. how does the monthly budget compare to actual experience?

1056. Are data elements reconcilable between internal summary reports and reports forwarded to the stakeholders?

1057. Are all cwbs elements specified for external reporting?

1058. Who are responsible for overhead performance control of related costs?

1059. Are meaningful indicators identified for use in measuring the status of cost and schedule performance?

1060. Do the rates and prices remain constant throughout the year?

1061. How do you identify and isolate causes of favorable and unfavorable cost and schedule variances?

1062. How do you identify potential or actual overruns and underruns?

1063. What are the actual costs to date?

1064. Are your organizations and items of cost assigned to each pool identified?

1065. Did a new competitor enter the market?

1066. Is data disseminated to the contractors management timely, accurate, and usable?

1067. Are there externalities from having some customers, even if they are unprofitable in the short run?

4.3 Earned Value Status: Time To Market

1068. How much is it going to cost by the finish?

1069. How does this compare with other Time To Market projects?

1070. What is the unit of forecast value?

1071. Where is evidence-based earned value in your organization reported?

1072. When is it going to finish?

1073. Are you hitting your Time To Market projects targets?

1074. Earned value can be used in almost any Time To Market project situation and in almost any Time To Market project environment. it may be used on large Time To Market projects, medium sized Time To Market projects, tiny Time To Market projects (in cut-down form), complex and simple Time To Market projects and in any market sector. some people, of course, know all about earned value, they have used it for years - but perhaps not as effectively as they could have?

1075. Validation is a process of ensuring that the developed system will actually achieve the stakeholders desired outcomes; Are you building the right product? What do you validate?

1076. Where are your problem areas?

1077. Verification is a process of ensuring that the developed system satisfies the stakeholders agreements and specifications; Are you building the product right? What do you verify?

1078. If earned value management (EVM) is so good in determining the true status of a Time To Market project and Time To Market project its completion, why is it that hardly any one uses it in information systems related Time To Market projects?

4.4 Risk Audit: Time To Market

1079. Is the number of people on the Time To Market project team adequate to do the job?

1080. Is the auditor able to evaluate contradictory evidence in an unbiased manner?

1081. Does willful intent modify risk-based auditing?

1082. Are procedures developed to respond to foreseeable emergencies and communicated to all involved?

1083. Extending the consideration on the halo effect, to what extent are auditors able to build skepticism in evidence review?

1084. Improving fraud detection: do auditors react to abnormal inconsistencies between financial and non-financial measures?

1085. What are the differences and similarities between strategic and operational risks in your organization?

1086. What does monitoring consist of?

1087. How will you maximise opportunities?

1088. Do your financial policies and procedures ensure that each step in financial handling (receipt, recording, banking, reporting) is not completed by one person?

1089. Are audit program plans risk-adjusted?

1090. Are there any forms the staff is required to sign?

1091. Does your organization have a process for meeting its ongoing taxation obligations?

1092. Have reasonable steps been taken to reduce the risks to acceptable levels?

1093. Are staff committed for the duration of the product?

1094. For paid staff, does your organization comply with the minimum conditions for employment and/or the applicable modern award?

1095. Does your auditor understand your business?

1096. Are your rules, by-laws and practices non-discriminatory?

4.5 Contractor Status Report: Time To Market

1097. How does the proposed individual meet each requirement?

1098. What was the overall budget or estimated cost?

1099. If applicable; describe your standard schedule for new software version releases. Are new software version releases included in the standard maintenance plan?

1100. Describe how often regular updates are made to the proposed solution. Are corresponding regular updates included in the standard maintenance plan?

1101. How is risk transferred?

1102. How long have you been using the services?

1103. What was the final actual cost?

1104. What was the budget or estimated cost for your organizations services?

1105. Are there contractual transfer concerns?

1106. What are the minimum and optimal bandwidth requirements for the proposed solution?

1107. Who can list a Time To Market project as organization experience, your organization or a previous employee of your organization?

1108. What was the actual budget or estimated cost for your organizations services?

1109. What process manages the contracts?

1110. What is the average response time for answering a support call?

4.6 Formal Acceptance: Time To Market

1111. Did the Time To Market project achieve its MOV?

1112. How does your team plan to obtain formal acceptance on your Time To Market project?

1113. Who would use it?

1114. Do you buy-in installation services?

1115. What function(s) does it fill or meet?

1116. Do you buy pre-configured systems or build your own configuration?

1117. Was the Time To Market project work done on time, within budget, and according to specification?

1118. What features, practices, and processes proved to be strengths or weaknesses?

1119. Does it do what Time To Market project team said it would?

1120. Is formal acceptance of the Time To Market project product documented and distributed?

1121. Was the client satisfied with the Time To Market project results?

1122. What can you do better next time?

1123. General estimate of the costs and times to complete the Time To Market project?

1124. Did the Time To Market project manager and team act in a professional and ethical manner?

1125. Was the Time To Market project goal achieved?

1126. Do you perform formal acceptance or burn-in tests?

1127. Who supplies data?

1128. Was the Time To Market project managed well?

1129. Was the sponsor/customer satisfied?

1130. What lessons were learned about your Time To Market project management methodology?

5.0 Closing Process Group: Time To Market

1131. What is the Time To Market project name and date of completion?

1132. What were things that you did well, and could improve, and how?

1133. What communication items need improvement?

1134. Was the schedule met?

1135. What is the overall risk of the Time To Market project to your organization?

1136. What were the desired outcomes?

1137. Were the outcomes different from the already stated planned?

1138. Was the user/client satisfied with the end product?

1139. How will staff learn how to use the deliverables?

1140. How well did you do?

1141. Were decisions made in a timely manner?

1142. What is the Time To Market project Management Process?

1143. Who are the Time To Market project stakeholders?

1144. Based on your Time To Market project communication management plan, what worked well?

1145. Can the lesson learned be replicated?

1146. What level of risk does the proposed budget represent to the Time To Market project?

1147. Will the Time To Market project deliverable(s) replace a current asset or group of assets?

1148. What will you do to minimize the impact should a risk event occur?

5.1 Procurement Audit: Time To Market

1149. Was the submission of variant tenders accepted and duly ruled?

1150. When tenders were actually rejected because they were abnormally low, were reasons for this decision given and were they sufficiently grounded?

1151. Are sub-criteria clearly indicated?

1152. If an electronic auction or a dynamic purchasing system was used, did the tender documents specify details on access to information, electronic equipment used and connection specifications?

1153. Was invitation to tender to each specific contract issued after the evaluation of the indicative tenders was completed?

1154. Is your organization policy on purchasing covered by a written manual?

1155. Was the decision on the award process accurate and adequately communicated?

1156. Do your organizations policies promote and/or safeguard fair competition?

1157. Are goods generally ordered and received in time to be used in the programs for which they were ordered?

1158. Were technical requirements set strict enough to guarantee the desired performance without being unnecessarily tight to exclude favourable bids that do not comply with all requirements?

1159. Has a deputy treasurer been appointed to sign checks when the treasurer is unable to perform that duty?

1160. Are eu procurement regulations applicable?

1161. How do you assess whether the technical and financial evaluation was done properly and in fair manner?

1162. Was the award criterion only the most economical advantageous tender?

1163. Was your organization specific about the nature and scope of the performance before launching the procurement process?

1164. Who is verifying the performance of the contract and approving payments?

1165. Is there a general policy on approval of purchases?

1166. Is there no evidence that the consultants participating in the Time To Market project design released information to contractors competing for the prime contract?

1167. Did the conditions included in the contract protect the risk of non-performance by the supplier and were there no conflicting provisions?

1168. Are transportation charges verified?

5.2 Contract Close-Out: Time To Market

1169. What is capture management?

1170. Change in circumstances?

1171. Change in knowledge?

1172. How is the contracting office notified of the automatic contract close-out?

1173. Have all contracts been closed?

1174. Have all contracts been completed?

1175. Was the contract sufficiently clear so as not to result in numerous disputes and misunderstandings?

1176. Have all acceptance criteria been met prior to final payment to contractors?

1177. Why Outsource?

1178. Was the contract type appropriate?

1179. Was the contract complete without requiring numerous changes and revisions?

1180. Are the signers the authorized officials?

1181. How does it work?

1182. Parties: Authorized?

1183. Parties: who is involved?

1184. Have all contract records been included in the Time To Market project archives?

1185. Has each contract been audited to verify acceptance and delivery?

1186. What happens to the recipient of services?

1187. How/when used ?

1188. Change in attitude or behavior?

5.3 Project or Phase Close-Out: Time To Market

1189. Planned completion date?

1190. What are the marketing communication needs for each stakeholder?

1191. Does the lesson educate others to improve performance?

1192. What is a Risk?

1193. How often did each stakeholder need an update?

1194. What stakeholder group needs, expectations, and interests are being met by the Time To Market project?

1195. What is a Risk Management Process?

1196. What is the information level of detail required for each stakeholder?

1197. Is there a clear cause and effect between the activity and the lesson learned?

1198. Planned remaining costs?

1199. What information did each stakeholder need to contribute to the Time To Market projects success?

1200. Which changes might a stakeholder be required to make as a result of the Time To Market project?

1201. What are the mandatory communication needs for each stakeholder?

1202. Who controlled key decisions that were made?

1203. In preparing the Lessons Learned report, should it reflect a consensus viewpoint, or should the report reflect the different individual viewpoints?

1204. Does the lesson describe a function that would be done differently the next time?

1205. Were risks identified and mitigated?

1206. Were cost budgets met?

1207. Is the lesson based on actual Time To Market project experience rather than on independent research?

5.4 Lessons Learned: Time To Market

1208. What is the growth stage of the organization?

1209. Who needs to learn lessons?

1210. Was Time To Market project performance validated or challenged?

1211. Are corrective actions needed?

1212. How effective was each Time To Market project Team member in fulfilling his/her role?

1213. How efficient were Time To Market project team meetings conducted?

1214. What would you approach differently next time?

1215. How effective were Time To Market project audits?

1216. What data are likely to be missing?

1217. How efficient is the deliverable?

1218. What is your organizational ideology?

1219. What on the Time To Market project worked well and was effective in the delivery of the product?

1220. How effective were your functional specs?

1221. What were the problems encountered in the

Time To Market project-functional area relationship, why, and how could they be fixed?

1222. How well did the scope of the Time To Market project match what was defined in the Time To Market project Proposal?

1223. What needs to be done over or differently?

1224. What are the expectations of the individuals?

1225. Were the right people available when required?

1226. What is your working hypothesis, if you have one?

Index

Printed in Poland
by Amazon Fulfillment
Poland Sp. z o.o., Wrocław

76465049R00193